MYSTERIES OF COBBLE HILL FARM

Pride, Prejudice, and Pitfalls

JOHNNIE ALEXANDER

Guideposts

A Gift from Guideposts

Thank you for your purchase! We want to express our gratitude for your support with a special gift just for you.

Dive into *Spirit Lifters*, a complimentary e-book that will fortify your faith, offering solace during challenging moments. Its 31 carefully selected scripture verses will soothe and uplift your soul.

Please use the QR code or go to **guideposts.org/spiritlifters** to download.

Mysteries of Cobble Hill Farm is a trademark of Guideposts.

Published by Guideposts
100 Reserve Road, Suite E200
Danbury, CT 06810
Guideposts.org

Copyright © 2025 by Guideposts. All rights reserved. This book, or parts thereof, may not be reproduced, stored in a retrieval system, or transmitted in any form or by any means, electronic, mechanical, photocopying, recording, or otherwise, without the written permission of the publisher.

This is a work of fiction. While the setting of Mysteries of Cobble Hill Farm as presented in this series is fictional, the location of Yorkshire, England, actually exists, and some places and characters may be based on actual places and people whose identities have been used with permission or fictionalized to protect their privacy. Apart from the actual people, events, and locales that figure into the fiction narrative, all other names, characters, businesses, and events are the creation of the author's imagination and any resemblance to actual persons or events is coincidental. Every attempt has been made to credit the sources of copyrighted material used in this book. If any such acknowledgment has been inadvertently omitted or miscredited, receipt of such information would be appreciated.

Scripture references are from the following sources: *The Holy Bible, King James Version* (KJV). *The Holy Bible, New International Version* (NIV). Copyright © 1973, 1978, 1984, 2011 by Biblica, Inc. Used by permission of Zondervan. All rights reserved worldwide. www.zondervan.com.

Cover and interior design by Müllerhaus
Cover illustration by Bob Kayganich at Illustration Online LLC.
Typeset by Aptara, Inc.

ISBN 978-1-961442-84-9 (hardcover)
ISBN 978-1-961442-85-6 (softcover)
ISBN 978-1-961442-86-3 (epub)

Printed and bound in the United States of America
10 9 8 7 6 5 4 3 2 1

MYSTERIES OF COBBLE HILL FARM

Pride, Prejudice, and Pitfalls

GLOSSARY OF UK TERMS

biscuit • cookie

car park • parking lot

cuppa • cup of tea

gimmer • young female sheep

loo • restroom

lorry • truck

pinderman • dogcatcher

telly • television

CHAPTER ONE

Harriet Bailey—now Harriet Bailey-Knight—listened intently as Garth Hamblin, playing the part of George Wickham, confided the injustices done to him after the death of his nemesis's father. They were seated next to each other on two straight-backed chairs, which were uncomfortable substitutes for a Victorian settee. Other residents of the White Church Bay community played quiet games of whist at two nearby card tables while those standing by the faux fireplace engaged in muted conversations.

"I do not wish to speak ill of the son," Garth said to Harriet, "despite his abominable treatment toward me. Though I can assure you that he will not hinder my enjoyment of such pleasant company as this evening has afforded. Should he be present at such gatherings, my behavior shall be in keeping with the decorum required by polite society. His elevated status will not keep me away."

"I'm glad to hear it." Harriet formed her lips into a smile that—she hoped—exuded Elizabeth Bennet's ladylike interest in George Wickham. Multiple times, she'd admitted that this acting business was more complicated than she'd expected.

At least this scene between Jane Austen's famed *Pride and Prejudice* protagonist and the charming son of the Pemberley estate's former steward wasn't too difficult to portray. Harriet genuinely liked Garth, a wildlife rehabilitation specialist for the nearby Yorkshire Coast Wildlife Centre. Their professional relationship had deepened into friendship a few months ago when they teamed up to find a rare pine marten that needed veterinary care.

The scenes that came later, after Elizabeth learns of Wickham's true nature, required Harriet to dig deeper into her limited acting repertoire. Showing polite scorn to Garth wasn't her major acting challenge, however. That came from pretending she felt nothing but contempt for the handsome Fitzwilliam Darcy.

In this amateur production, the role of Darcy, Pemberley's owner, was played by the handsome Fitzwilliam "Will" Knight.

The same man Harriet had married, in real life, only a couple of months before.

As Garth recited his next line, Lydia Bennet interrupted Elizabeth and Wickham's tête-à-tête. After delivering her sassy lines, Elena Hazeldine dragged Garth to downstage center, where other couples took their places for a lively jig.

As the lighting over the straight-backed chairs dimmed, Harriet relaxed and focused her gaze on Elena and Garth. Those two didn't need to feign their attraction, not when Elena practically glowed and Garth could barely take his eyes off her during the dance. The young widower, alone for several years, had shown no interest in giving away his heart again...until he'd met Elena. Now they were an official couple, with Jack, Elena's seven-year-old orphaned nephew, a very welcome third wheel.

Lost in her thoughts, Harriet startled when a woman plopped onto the chair beside her.

"I'm so glad I found you here." Poppy Schofield's stage whisper seemed to bounce to the front of the stage and back again.

Harriet placed her index finger against her lips. "We're rehearsing," she whispered.

Poppy's features scrunched together as she pointed to the dancers. "*They're* rehearsing. We're chatting in the corner like the two wallflowers we are. It's no different than if we were at the home of Mr. and Mrs. Phillips. Spectators instead of participants."

She breathed out a lingering sigh and rested her interlaced fingers on her tweed skirt. "Two unattached women longing for our knights in shining armor to give us our fairy-tale ending."

Harriet had barely squelched her amusement at Poppy's unexpected shift from scolding schoolmarm to dreamy romantic when a sharp elbow jabbed her in the ribs. "Though you already got your Knight, didn't you?"

"That I did," Harriet whispered as if she hadn't heard similar jokes a gazillion times in the past few months. She'd never tire of them, and she could already imagine relaying this conversation to Will later tonight. That was, if neither of them were called to any after-hours emergencies. Such was the life of a veterinarian married to a pastor.

A life they embraced, considering it a small price to pay for living it together.

Though they both wondered why their veterinary or pastoral emergencies couldn't happen on the same evenings instead of calling only one or the other away from home.

"It's such a blessing to have Pastor Will all married and settled. But I have to say I'm surprised you didn't sign up for any of the church's autumn bazaar committees." Poppy spoke without a hint of reproach, but the words stabbed Harriet all the same.

"Besides, everyone will expect to see you helping out," Poppy continued, "you being the pastor's wife and all. As much as we all love and appreciate Pastor Will, there's been a kind of emptiness in the church since the Cummingses left. Janice Cummings was such an energetic pastor's wife. It was often said she spent more time at the church than her husband did."

Harriet inwardly winced as Poppy's stage whisper increased in volume. She gestured to the nearby wing then stood and headed that way. Thankfully, Poppy followed.

Once she'd positioned herself so she could keep an eye on the play's director, who had the actors rehearsing the dance again, Harriet gave Poppy an apologetic smile. "Will and I already talked about my involvement with the bazaar. Because this is a busy time of year for the clinic, we decided I could help whenever I was free instead of signing up for a committee."

Poppy's lips turned downward as she appeared to process this strange idea. Perhaps strange to her mind, but Harriet thought it wise. It was October, and tupping season, the time when farmers put their rams and ewes together, was coming soon. Between now and then, Harriet needed to examine the farmers' stock to be sure they were in top condition for breeding and lambing. Those farm visits needed to be scheduled around her routine clinic appointments.

Before Poppy could respond, Harriet rushed on. "Aunt Jinny is on the banquet decorations committee, and Polly is in charge of the children's games. They both agreed I could pop in and out of their committee meetings as my time allowed. I already promised Aunt Jinny I would help with the table centerpieces in my free time."

Though any free time seemed to be a pipe dream at the moment.

"Jinny isn't even here," Poppy said. "Though I guess I shouldn't begrudge her an opportunity to visit Vienna."

Harriet's aunt had joined her son, a pharmacist who was attending a professional conference, and his wife, on the trip while his mother-in-law stayed with their seven-year-old twins. "She's having a great time sightseeing with Olivia. Anthony has been able to join them when his schedule allows. Besides, knowing Aunt Jinny, she already has a folder filled with decorating ideas for the banquet."

"The timing could have been better though."

"She didn't pick the dates for the conference," Harriet protested.

"I know that," Poppy replied with a girlish giggle. "It is what it is. Just like this play. Everyone is more interested in it than in making sure the bazaar is a success."

Harriet wasn't sure about that. Only about half of the people involved with the play attended White Church. The other half might attend the bazaar, but that would be their only involvement.

"That seems upside down to me, as if the bazaar isn't worth sacrificing something else for," Poppy continued. "Everyone claims to be so busy, but I'm busy too. You have no idea how early I get up to start my baking each morning, and yet I'm finding the time to supervise the entire bazaar."

Considering that the Biscuit Bistro, Poppy's adorable cookie shop located in White Church Bay's historic area, never opened before ten, Harriet had her doubts that Poppy's alarm was set much earlier than Harriet's own. Especially this time of year, when tourists were few and the shop opened for only a few hours a day during the week and closed on Sundays.

"Besides, being overworked or tired isn't an excuse when we're called to do the Lord's work." Poppy being Poppy, the rebuke was wrapped in cheer, as if it were one of her signature icing-covered shortbreads. "No one should know that better than the pastor's wife."

"I'm still a novice at being a pastor's wife." Surely even the incomparable Janice Cummings needed time—and the congregation's grace—before she became the embodiment of all the best qualities of the role.

"All I'm saying," Poppy replied, "is that using the clinic as an excuse seems especially odd when you've taken on one of the major roles in this play. Some people might wonder how you have time for rehearsals but no time to volunteer for the bazaar."

"Simple," Harriet said, even though there was more to her answer than she intended to share with Poppy. "I agreed to be in the play weeks before the autumn bazaar board held their first organizational meeting."

"But you were here last year. You must have known the bazaar is an annual event and in need of a multitude of hands."

Harriet swallowed a defeated sigh. Last year, she'd donated a trio of Cobble Hill Vet Clinic gift certificates for the banquet's silent auction and helped Will organize the teen talent show. No one had expected anything more from her than that. In fact, her small contributions to the event had been gushed over.

The congregation's expectations certainly had changed since she and Will exchanged their "I do's." At least five or six times in the past two months, someone had informed her about how Janice Cummings had done this or that.

"You should have seen the floral arrangements that Janice created for the vestibule. They were breathtaking."

"Was there anyone who could organize the volunteer appreciation dinner better than Janice?"

"No one ever worked harder than Janice on Spruce Up the Church Day."

No matter how often Will told Harriet not to take the not-quite-so-veiled criticisms to heart, she couldn't help feeling she wasn't measuring up in the eyes of her husband's congregants. Maybe she should officially join at least one committee, although she didn't know how she'd fit regular meetings into her already crowded schedule.

She'd even considered dropping out of the play. But Will had been adamant—if she wasn't Elizabeth, he wouldn't be Darcy. And they simply couldn't do that to Joel, Will's old friend. Though, perhaps, "former acquaintance" was a more apt description of their relationship. Joel Elphick, the director and new owner of the Beacon-on-the-Moor Playhouse, needed all the help he could get if his first production was to be a success.

The dance music faded, and Joel's voice resounded from the fourth row of theater seats. "Great job, everyone."

The auditorium lights came on over that section as he stood and flung out both arms as if to invite the entire cast into a virtual hug. He held a sheaf of papers attached to a clipboard in one hand, and the infamous red pen he used to scrawl his notes on each actor's performance in the other.

His neatly trimmed beard added maturity to his otherwise boyish features. However, these were accentuated by the crimson and gold soccer club ball cap hiding his prematurely receding hairline. Though no expert on male fashion, Harriet sensed Joel couldn't make up his mind about the persona he wanted to project to the world—that of the sophisticated artist or one of youthful exuberance.

Even his clothing, a tidy knitted sweater over a casual untucked shirt, seemed to send a mixed message. Or perhaps she was letting the little she knew of Joel's past unfairly influence her impression of him.

As Joel moved toward the front of the stage, Harriet touched the sleeve of Poppy's cardigan. "You'll have to excuse me. I need to hear what he has to say."

She joined the other actors gathering near the footlights, but apparently Poppy didn't intend to be dismissed so easily. Though she didn't have a role in the play, she scurried along behind Harriet.

"This is so exciting," she gushed. "A theater of our own being brought back to life again before our very eyes. My grandmother used to tell me stories of coming here when she was a girl. And every December she brought my mother to see *The Nutcracker*."

Poppy's excitement mellowed into wistfulness. "It was their holiday tradition. One Mother wished to share with me, but the Playhouse closed before I was old enough to sit through a ballet."

The amateur actress playing Mary Bennet, an older teen with round spectacles and brown hair pulled into a severe bun at the nape of her neck, glared at Poppy and Harriet.

"Do you mind?" she snarled before turning her back on them.

Red blotches colored Poppy's pale cheeks as she pressed her lips together. Harriet grimaced, regretting she hadn't somehow stopped Poppy's patter before "Mary" embarrassed her. On the flip side, at least now she could focus on what Joel was saying to the cast.

After a few constructive critiques to specific individuals, he stepped back with a wide smile. "We'll go through the scene one more time and then move on to the next one. Before you take your places, however, I want to say a special thank-you to a delightful woman who blesses all of us with her generosity and biscuit-baking skills. Several times a week, Poppy Schofield brings us treats from her shop without asking anything in return. Let's show her how much we appreciate her!"

Joel tucked the clipboard beneath his arm and clapped while a pleasant pink flush replaced the red blotchiness on Poppy's cheeks. Harriet pulled her into a side hug as the cast members clapped along with the director. Even "Mary" joined in, though without any enthusiasm.

When a few others approached Poppy to share a hug or express their personal thanks, Harriet moved out of the way. Joel caught her eye and winked, as if to answer her silent question. She nodded, certain now her suspicion that he'd overheard "Mary's" impolite reprimand was correct.

True, Poppy's incessant talking was impolite too. But only one of the two had been unkind. And that individual didn't share a name with a petite red flower.

As Harriet returned to the straight-backed chairs pretending to be a settee, she glanced at her watch. Once she-as-Elizabeth finished her brief conversation with Garth-as-Wickham, she would make a discreet exit and return to the clinic. Joel shouldn't mind, since she wasn't needed for the dance or for the next scene scheduled for rehearsal.

If neither she nor Garth flubbed their lines, she might have time to stop in at the church before heading to the clinic for her late-afternoon appointments. If Will had a few minutes, she'd tell him about Joel's charitable behavior toward Poppy. Even such a small interaction might help alleviate her husband's doubts about his friend's character. And reassure him that he was right to give Joel a second chance.

Harriet was about to take her seat when a bloodcurdling scream silenced all conversation and glued the actors' feet to the boards. A moment later, Kezia Ellsworth emerged from the stage-left curtains and stumbled toward Harriet.

The rail-thin woman practically collapsed before Harriet could grip her elbows and hold her steady. Her blue eyes, wide open and cold with fear, stared at Harriet.

"I—I saw—," Kezia stammered as tears streamed down her bloodless cheeks. "I saw a ghost."

CHAPTER TWO

Harriet guided the frightened woman to one of the straight-backed chairs and perched beside her. Within seconds, Joel knelt in front of Kezia and Garth encouraged the rest of the cast to stay a respectful distance away. Kezia gripped Harriet's hand between both of hers until it hurt. Harriet ignored the ache and maneuvered her free hand to check Kezia's pulse. Way too fast.

Joel shifted his gaze from Kezia to Harriet. "What happened? She looks like she might faint."

"You didn't hear what she said?"

"I was too far away."

Harriet glanced at Garth and the others gathered near him. Their puzzled expressions, mingled with concern, suggested they hadn't heard Kezia either.

If so, maybe Harriet had misunderstood. After all, there was no way Kezia could have seen a ghost. That was impossible—even for an early-nineteenth-century theater that had been abandoned for forty years.

A small cry escaped Kezia's lips. She released Harriet's hand and swiped away her tears. "Such a fuss I'm making. Over nothing, really." She seemed to force a too-broad smile. "The show must go on, as they say. I suppose that applies to rehearsals too."

As she rose to her feet, Harriet and Joel stood too, as if ready to catch her at a moment's notice.

"I think Charlotte Lucas can sit out one dance rehearsal," Joel said, referring to Kezia's character. "Perhaps someone could drive you home so you can rest."

"I can drive myself," Kezia said, indignation edging her tone. "I only live a few kilometers from here."

Joel frowned. "I don't think that's a good idea."

"Neither do I," Harriet added. "You've obviously had a fright. I can take you home." She turned to Joel. "That is, if you don't mind skipping over Elizabeth and Wickham's scene."

Joel glanced at the other cast members, clearly evaluating if someone besides Harriet could miss the rest of the day's rehearsal without causing too much disruption to his schedule. Harriet eyed the group too. Though she'd initially volunteered to drive Kezia out of kindness, her disappointment with Joel's hesitation revealed an ulterior motive.

She wanted to be alone with Kezia so she could find out what had happened. So many questions scurried around in her head. As Charlotte Lucas, Kezia danced with another cast member in the scene, so why had she left the stage during Joel's critique? Where was she when she saw this supposed ghost? What did the ghost look like?

Most important, what had frightened Kezia so much she'd almost fainted?

About the only thing Harriet loved more than all the "creatures great and small" she encountered at her clinic was a good mystery. Since she'd moved to Yorkshire from Connecticut after inheriting her grandfather's veterinary practice about eighteen months ago, she'd been involved in solving one odd mysterious puzzle after another. Something always seemed to be amiss in this quaint village and the surrounding countryside located next to high cliffs overlooking the North Sea.

"Poppy!" Joel called out in search of another volunteer, and Harriet's hope of a friendly chat with Kezia clunked to the floor. Within only a few minutes, and despite Kezia's objection, Joel had everything arranged. As soon as Poppy and Kezia were on their way, he instructed the cast to take their places and settled in his favorite spot.

Center seat, fourth row.

"That was an unexpected turn of events," Garth said as he joined Harriet on their pretend settee. "Kezia looked like she'd seen a ghost."

"She must have seen something." She graced him with her Elizabeth-smile and focused on delivering her opening line on Joel's cue. Though how she was supposed to focus on a tête-à-tête with Wickham when she longed for a tête-à-tête with Kezia, she didn't have a clue.

The glorious oranges, reds, and golds of October's leaves were resplendent against the pale blue of the late afternoon sky. They waved and danced as the cold breezes blew in from the nearby North Sea. This time of year, the sun set shortly before six. Already, with a little over two hours still to go, the dim sunlight cast lengthening shadows across the Cobble Hill Farm grounds.

Harriet parked her Land Rover, a utilitarian vehicle she affectionately called the Beast, in front of the clinic between two other cars. The Citroën Picasso, with its cute color name of "blue flair," belonged to Polly Worthington, née Thatcher, the spunky twenty-five-year-old receptionist who stayed on after Harriet's grandfather's death. The other vehicle must belong to the clinic's newest client.

Who was fifteen minutes early.

Good thing Harriet had decided against stopping at the church to see Will after she left the theater.

She shut off the Beast's ignition then rubbed the back of her neck. The clinic's normal weekday hours were from eight to four with time blocked off as necessary for farm calls. Because of today's rehearsal schedule, Polly had scheduled all the afternoon appointments between four and six.

Since the Cobble Hill Vet Clinic was located in one wing of her stone Georgian-style home, Harriet decided to take a few more minutes to herself before putting on her veterinarian's hat. She followed the landscaped pathway to the front of the 1820s house, which faced the North Sea, and opened the door into the tastefully decorated foyer.

How much she loved this old house with its family antiques, comforting creaks, and treasured memories. During her childhood, she and her parents had made frequent trips from their Connecticut home to visit her grandparents. Moving to White Church Bay after her grandfather's death was almost like settling into her second home. Not that she hadn't experienced moments of culture shock or bouts of homesickness from time to time. But after all this time—a delightful and blessed year-and-a-half—she definitely *belonged*.

In this house. On this farm. With this community.

Dare she say, even in England?

Why not? As Elizabeth Bennet, a gentleman's daughter, might have said under such circumstances, Harriet was the daughter of an Englishman, thus half-English herself. And she'd married a proper Englishman. Now they shared this historic home together, which only gave Harriet more reason to love the place.

As she shut the front door, Maxwell scurried to her as fast as a dog with wheels for back legs could run. The black-and-tan long-haired dachshund's hindquarters were paralyzed after he was hit by a car a few years ago. A local boy who saw the accident brought him to the clinic, where Grandad treated the injuries and eventually had him fitted with a wheeled prosthesis.

"That dog's got more fight in him than a heavyweight champion," he'd told Harriet when he introduced her to Maxwell. "Since no one's come to claim him, this is his home now as much as it is mine."

After Harriet dropped her bag and jacket on a nearby bench, she knelt to greet the sweet dachshund. "You having a good day? Mine's been a bit crazy." While she told him about Kezia's ghost, she checked the prosthesis straps then scratched Maxwell behind the ears.

"Someone's waiting on me," she said as she stood. "A Chihuahua who's new to the neighborhood, if I'm remembering right. You want to come to the clinic with me?"

Maxwell's enthusiastic yip definitely meant *yes*. He followed Harriet into the kitchen, where she paused for a drink of water, then through the door leading into the clinic. After Harriet slipped into her emerald-green smock, Maxwell trotted beside her to the lobby.

With a last flick of his tail, he disappeared beneath Polly's workstation to settle into his plush bed.

Harriet glanced at the empty chairs in the waiting area then exchanged a quick greeting with Polly. Broad russet swathes, perfect for autumn, highlighted her receptionist's dark shoulder-length hair.

"I put teeny-tiny Gizmo and his not-so-tiny dad—meaning he's a tall bloke—in exam room one when I caught sight of the Beast passing by the door." Polly handed over the patient folder. "How was rehearsal?"

"Interesting." Even though they were alone, Harriet leaned over the counter and lowered her voice. "Kezia Ellsworth told me she saw a ghost."

Polly's eyes narrowed. "Practical, no-nonsense Kezia? That doesn't sound like her."

"Right? She practically fainted, so something definitely frightened her." Harriet straightened as a beep sounded.

Polly tapped a button on her phone. "That's my reminder to get up and stretch. Gotta get those steps in if I want to lose these newlywed kilograms."

Harriet grinned and rolled her eyes. Polly and Van discovered a love for cooking meals together after their marriage, and both complained of putting on a few pounds, though certainly not enough for Harriet to even notice.

"I'll also take it as my cue to go to work," she said. "I'll tell you about Kezia as soon as I'm done with Gizmo."

"Don't count on it." Polly tapped the folders beside her computer as she stood. "We've got a busy couple of hours ahead of us."

"Which will make the time fly." A small and much appreciated blessing, especially when Harriet was eager to spend a quiet evening at home with her husband and their little menagerie.

Thanks to Polly's efficient scheduling and assistance, Harriet gave each of her patients her complete attention while she moved back and forth between the two exam rooms. Throughout the rest of the afternoon, she took vital signs, listened to heartbeats, gave inoculations, treated an ear infection, and recommended surgery for an abscessed tooth.

She smiled broadly as she rapped on the door then entered exam room two for her last and most anticipated appointment of the day. Rand Cromwell, the local pinderman, a Yorkshire term for dogcatcher that Harriet found delightful, had brought in his beloved Sahara for a routine health check. Six months ago, Rand found the malnourished spaniel mix with a rope embedded in her neck after an anonymous individual called in a neglect report.

As the door opened, Rand stood, and Sahara, who was sprawled at his feet, wagged her tail.

"You beautiful girl," Harriet gushed as she lowered herself to the floor and held out a hand. "Always the careful one, aren't you? Nothing wrong with that."

Sahara stood and took cautious steps toward Harriet and sniffed her fingers. Her long, feathery tail increased its back-and-forth momentum, and a moment later she rested her muzzle against Harriet's cheek.

"It might take her a minute," Rand said, "but my Sahara never forgets those who've done right by her."

Harriet gently rubbed one of Sahara's silky ears between her fingers while running her other hand along the dog's back. The dog had gained much-needed weight since her last visit to the clinic, and her coat, once a matted mess, had grown in with a healthy sheen. The only reminder of her horrendous experience was the scars around her neck, though those were mostly hidden by her fur.

"You've done wonders with her, Rand. Not that I'm surprised." The bond between the dogcatcher and the mistreated dog had been instantaneous and strong. And obviously lasting.

During the examination, which began with a delicate probing of the scar tissue, Harriet asked Rand routine questions about Sahara's diet, general health, and temperament. To hear Rand talk, she was the perfect companion.

"She goes to work with me every day," he said, "and just about everywhere else too. She's still a little shy around strangers, but not as much as she used to be. And she's a fast learner. Real quick to pick up on things."

"You've given her confidence." Harriet gave Sahara a pumpkin-flavored treat. "And she knows she can trust you to keep her safe."

"That I do. I'll never let anyone treat her like rubbish that's good for nothin' but the bin ever again. When I look back on that day, it seems like the Good Lord put us together, and I sure am glad He did."

"So am I." Harriet placed her hands on either side of Sahara's sweet face and gazed into the warmth of her dark brown eyes. Moments like this one, that so clearly showed the value of the work she'd devoted her life to, filled her heart with an amazing sense of joyful peace. Grandad had paved her path with his compassion for the animals in his care. Like Maxwell, whose paralysis and other injuries made life difficult for him. Some might have said too difficult.

But Grandad didn't let the severity of the dachshund's injuries stop him from doing everything he could to provide healing and comfort. And now Harriet couldn't imagine life without the sweet little guy's comedic antics.

The same with Charlie, the muted calico cat with the ageless yellow eyes. She was the latest in a line of office cats Grandad had christened "Charlie" regardless of gender, and she'd suffered a cruel tragedy as a kitten. A Good Samaritan had rescued her from a burning trash can, and her body still bore the scars from the fire amid her patches of gray, ginger, and white fur. Because of the round-the-clock care Grandad had given her when she arrived at the clinic, Charlie now lived a pampered, carefree life.

Thankfully, Sahara's story wasn't as dire as Maxwell's or Charlie's. What truly mattered, though, was that she now had someone to love and care for her.

Harriet stole a glance at Rand, who only had eyes for his dog. The solitary pinderman obviously needed the gentle spaniel mix as much as she needed him. Harriet's heart filled with gratitude for the small role that God had given her to play in Rand and Sahara's story.

Those warm fuzzies stayed with her as Rand settled his account with Polly. Once he and Sahara left, Harriet threw her arms out wide.

"I love my life," she exclaimed.

Polly laughed at the unexpected declaration then tilted her head. "Does this have anything to do with wedded bliss? Because I also love mine."

Her gray eyes sparkled as she picked up a framed photo then held it beside her cheek as if modeling it. The picture showed Polly, looking absolutely gorgeous in a pale pink dress with lacy cap sleeves, standing next to Detective Constable Van Worthington. Their expressions exuded joy and hope. The photo had been taken on Polly's cell phone moments after the eloping couple said their vows. Their surprise wedding took place only a few weeks before Harriet and Will exchanged their own vows.

"Wedded bliss is wonderful," Harriet replied to Polly's question. "But at this moment, I was thinking about Rand and Sahara. She was such a mess when he and Van brought her in that I wasn't sure we could save her. But now she's a beautiful, happy dog." Once again, warm fuzzies filled Harriet's heart.

She'd known from a young age, on a farm call she went on with Grandad, that she wanted to be a veterinarian. Never once had she wavered from that firm certainty or regretted her vocational choice. Providing veterinary care was much more than her profession—it was who she was in the deepest depths of her spirit, as if God had knitted within her DNA the compassion, empathy, and skills she'd need to care for the furred, feathered, shelled, and slimy.

"Sahara's lucky to have you as her vet," Polly said, breaking into Harriet's thoughts. She returned the frame to the desk, placing it beside another photograph of Van and among the other tchotchkes arranged near her computer. "And you seem less harried than when you arrived. What was all that about a ghost?"

Harriet related what had happened at the rehearsal.

"Are you sure no one else heard what Kezia said?"

"I'm pretty sure. I wish I could have been the one to drive her home."

"I wish you could have too." Polly retrieved her bag from a desk drawer then dug out her keys in preparation to close the office. "When do you expect to see her again?"

"Unfortunately, Charlotte Lucas isn't in many scenes, so Kezia doesn't come to every rehearsal."

"Nothing says you can't call on her. Let her know you're concerned."

"I am concerned." Harriet frowned. Even she could hear the lack of conviction in her words. She took a deep breath. "Honest, I am. But I have to confess, I'm mostly curious. We know she didn't see a ghost. But whatever she saw frightened her half to death. What do you suppose it could have been?"

"I wouldn't discard the ghost theory so quickly," Polly said, a teasing lilt to her voice. "After all, this is the spooky season. And where better to find a ghost than an old abandoned theater?"

"It's not abandoned anymore," Harriet asserted. Joel had spent a considerable amount of money on cleaning and refurbishing the main areas such as the lobby, auditorium, and stage. But there was still a great deal to be done, including part of the backstage area and the upper story. The general contractor that he'd hired was often onsite to oversee the ongoing construction plus the much-needed electrical and plumbing upgrades.

"Maybe so." Polly bent to say goodbye to Maxwell then rounded her desk. "But Kezia Ellsworth is one of the most sensible, practical people I know. She's the perfect Charlotte Lucas."

Polly had a point—the same one Harriet herself had considered.

"Besides," Polly added as she shrugged into her jacket, "mysterious things have happened there before."

Harriet's curiosity meter immediately went on full alert. "What kinds of mysterious things?"

"It was a place we avoided as kids because of stories of strange lights and other goings-on. It was probably nothing more than older kids hanging out there. But almost every historic theater in England comes with a ghost story. Why should the Beacon-on-the-Moor Playhouse be any different?"

CHAPTER THREE

The frozen lasagna that Polly had put in the oven for Harriet in between veterinary appointments only needed to bake for ten more minutes. So where was Will?

Harriet tapped her phone to light up the screen. Still no response to her text. Which meant he didn't have access to his phone, or he was in what he called an "uninterruptible situation." Either way, there was no use calling him, since he obviously couldn't answer.

Her only other option was to call the church office, but Claire Marshall, the church administrator, would have left for the day over an hour ago.

"There might be someone around who'd answer a ringing telephone," Harriet said to Maxwell, who was taking the last bites of his own supper. "But what good would it do? I don't want to bother him if he can't be bothered. He'll be here when he gets here, and we need to be patient. And keep the lasagna from burning."

During their dating days, Harriet and Will had plenty of practice making the best of interrupted plans or rearranging schedules at the last minute. Though she was disappointed her evening hadn't gone as she'd hoped, Will's evening probably wasn't going as he'd hoped either. Thankfully, they'd have plenty of quiet dinners in the years ahead. Hundreds and hundreds of them.

She pulled the steaming lasagna out of the oven and set it on the counter. When Will arrived home she'd pop it back in again along with the garlic bread.

The salad was made, the table set, and the candles ready to be lit, so Harriet wandered into the reading nook. This cozy alcove, located at one side of the foyer, had been a favorite refuge since she was a girl. Because the only seating was one upholstered wingchair, neither she nor Will spent much time in the room these days.

Their loss was the cats' gain.

Charlie and Ash Wednesday, the gray kitten from an abandoned litter that Will adopted several months ago, were tangled together in the comfy wingchair. Not wanting to disturb their sleep, Harriet wandered across the hall into Grandad's study.

Like the reading nook, nothing in this long, rectangular room had changed since Will moved in. Actually, very little had changed since Harriet moved in.

Grandad's desk, his books, journals, and keepsakes were all still there. Along with so many of her childhood memories. In the entire house, this was where she felt closest to the man who'd been not only a beloved grandfather but her mentor and her hero.

She dropped into the wide leather chair behind the spacious desk and opened the email app on her phone to check her inbox. Within minutes, a text popped up from Will.

Leaving church soon. Just got a text from Joel. Would you mind if I asked him to join us for supper? He sounds like a man in need of a good home-cooked meal. Will explain more later.

The message was followed by another with a long line of heart and bouquet emojis.

"No candlelight dinner tonight," Harriet murmured. But at least Will would be home soon, and he must have a good reason for wanting to invite Joel or he wouldn't have asked if she minded. She had enough food prepared for unexpected company, and the house was clean except for a quick tidy-up in the kitchen.

She quickly tapped out her reply: HE'S MOST WELCOME TO JOIN US. HURRY HOME!

As she headed to the dining room to replace the tapered candles with an autumn spice jarred candle, she sent a second text to reassure Will that she understood such last-minute ministry opportunities sometimes happened, particularly in a pastor's life. THANK YOU SO MUCH FOR CHECKING WITH ME FIRST!

By the time she'd popped the lasagna and garlic bread into the oven, added another place setting to the table, and tossed the salad, Will had arrived. He greeted Harriet with a kiss then launched into his apology.

"Sorry I didn't text you sooner. I accidentally left my phone in my office when I went out on a ministry call and didn't even realize it until I got back in the car."

"No apology needed," Harriet replied, her hands clasped behind his neck. "Where's Joel?"

"He'll be here any minute. He'd texted to see if we could get together this evening. When I called him, he sounded a little off." Will's lips curved into the apologetic smile that never failed to weaken Harriet's knees. "Inviting him to dinner seemed the right thing to do even though it messed up our plans for a quiet evening."

"It did, but you were right to ask him to come over." Harriet leaned in to give Will a peck on the cheek then pulled a decanter of chilled water from the fridge. "Did he tell you what happened at rehearsal?"

"He didn't really tell me anything except it'd been a long and strange day." The front doorbell chimed. "That should be him."

While Will opened the door for their guest, Harriet filled the water glasses.

"Something smells wonderful," Joel said as he preceded Will into the kitchen. "I appreciate the invite. Otherwise, it'd be beans on toast in front of the telly for me tonight."

The trio engaged in small talk as they settled at the dining room table. After Will said grace, Joel seemed to steer the conversation away from anything that had to do with today's rehearsal. In fact, it felt to Harriet as if he didn't want to talk about the theater at all.

Instead, he shared anecdotes about his life before his move to White Church Bay. As Harriet already knew, he and Will had both lived for a time in Foxglove End, the same southern English village where Will once held what was called a "two-church charge." The two men, both single and of prime marital age, were popular in the rural area, where a decidedly older demographic lived.

The women invited them to dinners and outings when granddaughters and nieces came to visit. Their husbands took them to their hidden fishing spots, insisted they join the local cricket team, and regaled them, at every gathering, with exaggerated stories of their own youths.

Aside from their social interactions, Will and Joel spent little time together. Joel was an infrequent church attendee, and Will was too busy shepherding two churches to accompany Joel on his weekend excursions around the countryside. Especially since he was never quite sure when Joel's reckless side would overpower his common sense.

Will had confided to Harriet that the man was a conundrum. At times, Joel seemed to be searching for a rock to hold on to, for the peace that passes understanding. But a childhood tragedy—his adoptive parents died in a car accident when he was a young teen—appeared to hinder his efforts to fully trust in God's love for him.

They hadn't stayed in touch after Will moved to White Church Bay. Joel had spent the past several years directing classic theater productions throughout England.

Then one day, out of the blue, a solicitor contacted him with the news that he'd been offered ownership of the Beacon-on-the-Moor Playhouse by an anonymous benefactor who admired his work. No strings attached except one—that his first production would be Jane Austen's *Pride and Prejudice*, the same play that was being performed when the theater closed forty years before.

Joel readily agreed.

When he arrived in White Church Bay five or six months ago, Harriet and Will hosted a small party to introduce him to their friends and organized volunteers to help with cleaning the building before the major work could begin.

Joel began the casting process even before the first phase of the major renovations neared completion. He insisted that Will and Harriet try out for the parts of Fitzwilliam Darcy and Elizabeth Bennet.

Harriet thought she was too old for the part of the not yet one-and-twenty-year-old, especially when Polly was chosen for the role of Jane, Elizabeth's older sister. Joel had assured Harriet that presence counted for more than youth for this particular role. With Joel's urging and Will's encouragement, she'd finally agreed.

After their leisurely meal, Will and Joel cleared the table while Harriet dished up generous squares of old-fashioned Yorkshire parkin, an oatmeal-gingerbread cake. She warmed the slices and topped each with a scoop of vanilla ice cream.

"Is that what I think it is?" Joel asked as he eyed the dessert. "I haven't had parkin since I was a lad in knickers."

Will chuckled. "You were never a lad in knickers."

"See? It's been way too long."

"No need to wait another minute then." Harriet slid a dessert plate across the kitchen island toward him then gestured to a stool. "Let's just stay right here in the kitchen. Go ahead and have a seat."

Without a moment's hesitation, Joel slipped onto the stool and took a large bite of the sticky spice cake. "This is absolutely delicious, Harriet. Takes me straight back to my childhood."

"Then I wish I could take credit for it, but I have no idea how to make it. Fern Chapman, our indomitable Lady Catherine de Bourgh, gave it to me this morning when I went to her farm to check on her goat. She made the cake a couple of days ago, but she said this is one of those odd desserts that gets better with age."

"So that's the secret. Two-day-old cake. I love it." Joel took another bite, and Harriet also chose a seat at the island. Once he swallowed, he waved his fork toward Harriet. "Wait a minute. Do you mean to tell me you were treating goats before you came to rehearsal today?"

"One goat. Fern's favorite, even though he gets into the most mischief of any goat in Yorkshire."

"I think that's why he's her favorite," Will chimed in as he prepared a pot of tea to accompany their dessert.

Harriet nodded her agreement as she took her first bite of the cake. Joel was right—it was absolutely delicious. Though she didn't consider her palate to be all that refined, she definitely tasted ginger and dark molasses. And Fern had told her that a smattering of oats gave the cake a delightful texture.

When Joel finished his last bite, he turned to Harriet with a sheepish grin and held his plate out with both hands. "Please, ma'am, may I have some more?" he said in a plaintive tone as his eyes pleaded for her to say yes.

At his spot-on impression of Oliver Twist, the orphan from Charles Dickens's novel of the same name, Will enthusiastically clapped, and Harriet placed another parkin square on Joel's plate. While she added a scoop of ice cream, Joel stood and gave an exaggerated bow then returned to his seat.

"I played that part more times than I can count as a kid," he said. "Nice to know that line still works."

"Or you could have just asked for seconds," Will teased. "Like I'm doing."

"And miss a golden opportunity to perform? Never!" Joel lifted his teacup as if making a toast. "I need to thank Fern personally next time I see her. She's seldom at the theater, since we haven't rehearsed any of the de Bourgh scenes recently. But even at the auditions, I remember thinking she was perfect for the role. She's someone with a mind of her own and that special kind of aristocratic gravitas that makes her performance so authentic."

"I especially agree with her having a mind of her own," Will said as they lingered over their tea. "Believe it or not, you're seeing the mellowed version of our Fern. Harriet has been a good influence on her."

"I'm not sure about that," Harriet protested. "Though I agree Fern is no longer as abrasive as the first time I had to save that silly goat from himself."

The conversation turned from that unfortunate incident, when the goat tangled himself in a spare roll of barbed wire he'd found behind a shed, to anecdotes about crazy encounters Harriet had experienced with other animals and their owners. She mentioned to Will that Rand and Sahara had come in that afternoon then shared their story with Joel.

"You do more than heal cats and dogs," he said. "You give people happiness."

"Yes, she does." Will squeezed Harriet's hand, and she responded with a warm smile.

"You're both giving me too much credit, and I thank you. But that's enough clinic talk." She let out a breath then focused on Joel. "I was wondering if you talked to Kezia since she left rehearsal. I considered giving her a call but..." She regretted she hadn't done so while waiting for Will to come home. Now it was too late.

Harriet met Will's questioning gaze. "Something frightened her so badly that Poppy had to drive her home."

"I went by her house after rehearsal," Joel said. "She was lying down, so I didn't see her. Andrew said she needed to rest but she'd be at tomorrow night's rehearsal."

He focused his gaze on Harriet. "What did she say to you when she stumbled in from the wings?"

Harriet toyed with the last bite of parkin on her plate as she considered how to answer. On the one hand, as owner of the theater and the director of the production, he had a right to know. On the other, once Kezia had gotten over her initial fright, she obviously hadn't wanted to repeat what she'd told Harriet.

She took a deep breath and folded her hands in her lap. "I'll tell you what she said. But this has to stay between us. I don't want Kezia to be embarrassed by any crazy gossip that might get spread around."

Harriet frowned. "Though Polly already knows. I told her when I returned to the clinic. And she probably told Van. But they won't say anything to anyone else."

"You can count on me," Joel said. "I don't much care for gossip. What happened?"

Harriet took a deep breath then blurted, "She said she saw a ghost."

Will's eyes rounded, and Joel startled. He opened his mouth, but no words came out.

"She didn't describe what she saw," Harriet said. "I thought she was going to faint, so I led her to a chair. As everyone else came around to see what was going on, she completely shut down."

Joel made a weird choking noise, a cross between clearing his throat and a cough. When he spoke, tension edged his voice. "I didn't hear her say anything about a ghost."

"I promise that's what she said." Harriet shifted her gaze to Will. "I don't know if I've ever seen someone so fearful."

Suddenly Joel stood, placed his hands on his head, and paced in a circle behind his stool. "This can't be happening. On top of everything else—" He pressed his lips shut and closed his eyes, as if needing a moment to pull himself together.

Harriet could practically read Will's thoughts as he met her gaze. He'd told her about Joel's tendency to make mountains out of molehills when they'd known each other before. His exaggerations had caused a few kerfuffles that required Will to take on the role of peacemaker. But his most egregious offense had been promoting an investment scheme that went belly-up. Will hadn't given Joel any money. However, those people who did lost everything.

Joel lost money too—at least he claimed he did—but Will wasn't sure if that was true. As much as he wanted to trust Joel now, to give him the benefit of the doubt and help him with this new venture, Harriet knew her husband didn't fully trust Joel's integrity.

"What does that mean?" Though Will spoke softly, his tone was firm. "Harriet and I are your friends. You can tell us what's going on."

Joel, his fingers locked behind his head, took in a deep breath then exhaled. He dropped his arms to his sides and rolled his shoulders as if to relieve himself of his burden. Yet the pained expression on his face indicated the weight still pressing on him.

"I'm not sure where to begin," he said, the words brimming with defeat.

"Wherever you're comfortable," Will replied. Those few words, simple as they might be, stirred Harriet's heart. His gift for making others feel that their troubles were more important to him than anything else at that moment had impressed her when she first met him. People trusted him, and he honored that trust with his wisdom and discretion.

"Okay then." Joel returned to the stool and placed his hands around his teacup. "First there's the theater itself. It seems every week an issue I thought was resolved...isn't. If Piers Berrycloth didn't have such a great reputation..." He shook his head. "I know you think the world of him, but sometimes I can't help but wonder if he's sabotaging me."

Harriet held her tongue, though everything within her screamed to defend Piers. She'd hired the local contractor for various projects for the house, the clinic, and the other buildings on the Cobble Hill property. He'd especially done a great job upgrading the electrical system in the barn that she sometimes used to board her clients' pets. Whenever a problem arose at the church or the parsonage, Piers volunteered his expertise to make sure the job was done right and with as little expense as possible.

"I'm not accusing him of anything nefarious," Joel hurried to say, as if sensing Harriet's sudden tension. "You know how much I want to contribute to this community. For people to feel like the Beacon belongs to them as much as it does to me. Hiring local contractors and carpenters and landscapers helps make that happen."

He paused and gave Will a rueful look. "As much as I hate to say it, Piers may be in over his head. Sometimes I regret I didn't hire that large contracting company in Whitby. Then I might have known about all these electrical and plumbing problems at the beginning that are popping up now. Every two or three days, it's something new."

"Since the problems need to be fixed regardless of when they're found, would knowing more details up front have saved you money?" Will asked.

"Probably not," Joel admitted. "Though I might have made different decisions on other expenses if these unexpected issues had been identified before we started on the upgrades."

For a moment or two, both men seemed lost in their own thoughts. Harriet supposed Joel was brooding over his financial woes, while Will wanted to be prudent in his responses. She was puzzled, however, by Joel's reaction to what Kezia had said. As if her claiming to see a ghost somehow hurt him or the theater.

"I don't understand why this is a problem. There are 'haunted' theaters all over England," she said, using her fingers to trace air quotes. "Wouldn't it just make the theater more intriguing to people?"

Joel's eyes widened. "You can't believe Kezia saw a ghost."

"Of course, I don't. None of us do," Harriet assured him. "There aren't ghosts in those other theaters, either, but that hasn't stopped people from talking about them. Or visiting the theaters for the fun of a ghost tour."

"You're right," Joel conceded. He frowned as he lowered his eyes and cracked his knuckles.

"That's a sure sign something else is bothering you." Will pointed to Joel's interlocked fingers then turned to Harriet and lowered his voice as if sharing a secret. "He doesn't even realize he's doing it."

A sheepish grin lifted Joel's features then faded. He dug in his jeans pocket and pulled out a folded piece of crumpled paper. "I found this on my windshield after rehearsal this evening. It's not the first."

He flipped the paper across the island to Will, who opened the note and read it to himself. His jaw muscle clenched, and he narrowed his eyes. When he handed the note to Harriet, she braced herself for what must be bad news.

It was worse than she'd thought. The typed words read:
You ignore my warnings at your own peril. I know who you are and what you've done. You're not welcome here.

"Who wrote this?" Horrified by the words, Harriet read them to herself again. "What are you supposed to have done?"

"Nothing to warrant a threat like this." Joel worked his mouth, and his eyes clouded as he looked at Will. "I'll be the first to admit I've made some stupid mistakes in my life. And I've hurt a lot of people." He lowered his head.

Harriet darted a glance at Will, who said to Joel, "Take your time."

Joel took a deep breath. "I've done things I'm not proud of. Taken advantage of people. Cheated people who considered me a friend. Always looking out for number one—that was me. But all that changed a few years ago." He pressed his hand against his chest. "I've changed. And I've made amends wherever I could."

"I'm glad to hear that," Will said. "And it's true. You are different. I can see it."

"You've always been a fine chap." A sad smile tugged at Joel's mouth. "Even when I didn't deserve your friendship. You should know that the seeds you planted all those years ago in Foxglove End eventually took root. When I found out you were the minister here, in the same little village where I'd purchased an old run-down theater, I was stunned. And then I thanked God for such a blessed surprise."

"I thank Him too," Will said. "Harriet and I are glad God led you to our little corner of Yorkshire."

"Me too. Though I'm not sure why He did when I've run into one obstacle after another."

Will blew out a breath, then his features relaxed into a compassionate smile. "'Though He slay me, yet will I trust in Him.'"

"I'm familiar with that one." Joel's shoulders straightened, and he cleared his throat as if preparing to give a recitation. "Job 13:15. The grieving, pain-afflicted Job, unaware of the spiritual contest between God and Satan, is responding to one of his so-called friends."

Joel shifted toward Harriet. "I happened to be in church when Will preached a sermon about Job's trust in God despite all the calamity happening around him. I never forgot it. These days, I remind myself that at least I'm not covered in boils."

Harriet chuckled at his joke. His troubles with the theater were a legitimate concern. But the threatening note was an even greater one.

She gestured to the paper she still held in her hand. "You said this wasn't the first. What did the others say?"

"One said, 'Go away.' Another, 'You'll never make it here.' And then there was my favorite, 'This county isn't big enough for both of us, and I was here first.'"

"That's so..." Harriet searched for the right word and finally settled on one. "Childish."

"Tell me about it." Joel poured more tea in his cup, took a sip, and made a face.

Will immediately stood and reached for the kettle. "I'll brew a fresh pot."

"Please don't," Joel said. "At least not on my account. I should be getting home."

"What about the notes?" Harriet asked. "What did you do with them? Have you told Van?"

"I threw the first two away. They seemed so ridiculous, I hardly gave them a second thought. I still have the third one, though I hate to bother Van when all I have is typed words on scraps of paper."

"I think you should tell him." Harriet turned to Will. "Don't you agree?"

"Are you aware there are rumors going around about you?" Will asked Joel instead of answering Harriet.

Her eyes widened in surprise at this news. She hadn't heard anything negative about Joel at all.

"The one about me not paying my bills and being on the verge of bankruptcy?" Joel shook his head. "It's not true. Sure, I need to be frugal, and I'm taking a risk with the Beacon. But I'll cut my losses before I bail out on my financial obligations. I promise you that."

"How does a rumor like that get started?" Harriet asked.

"Probably by the same person who wrote that." Will nodded to the note in Harriet's hand. "I agree with Harriet. You should report this to Van. And if you get another one, try not to handle it too much. There might be a fingerprint on it."

"Guess I should have thought of that." Joel stood and stacked his teacup and saucer onto his dessert plate. Harriet stopped him with a quick assurance that they'd take care of clearing up and gave him back the note.

Together, she and Will walked Joel to the door and saw him off. Afterward, as they tidied the dining room and kitchen, Harriet had a disturbing thought.

What if whoever was threatening Joel decided the notes weren't enough? What else might that person do to get Joel to leave White Church Bay?

Journal Entry
April 14, 2025

It's done. The final promise, made so very long ago, has been kept. Forgive me, dear friend, that it took so long for me to give him your gift. My expectation, and perhaps yours, was that he'd receive it when he graduated from university. So often I imagined him in his cap and gown. How proud we'd be!

But he didn't deserve it then.

It breaks my heart to write those words. It broke my heart to see your precious son, that beautiful little boy who brought such joy to his adoptive parents, experience such heartbreaking grief at their loss. I didn't know how to help him and dared not get close to him.

So I stayed in the shadows and prayed for your child during his difficult years. God was gracious and answered my prayers.

That tiny baby you once held in your arms is a man now. A good man with a good heart. He will value your gift.

CHAPTER FOUR

Harriet patted the final ewe on the rump as Malachi Atkins released it from the chute. The elderly farmer's small flock of sheep was the last one on Friday morning's "getting ready for tupping" rotation. The single ram and the dozen ewes had easily passed Harriet's health checklist. They were at optimal weights with no signs of infections or disease.

"Barring any delivery complications," Harriet said, "you should have quite a few lambs playing in your pasture come spring."

"Since none of my ewes are gimmers, I'm expectin' at least twenty." Mr. Atkins's green eyes gleamed with satisfaction. "For the past couple of years, I've only kept the ones that birth twins or triplets. And of those the ones who are the best mamas."

Harriet smiled her approval of his business plan. A gimmer, a term she'd learned as a young girl while visiting farms with her grandfather, was a young female sheep.

Mr. Atkins picked up Harriet's veterinary bag. "You'll come into the house for a cuppa. The missus is baking this morning, so there's sure to be somethin' warm and tasty on the table."

Only rarely did Harriet refuse Mr. Atkins's invitation to enjoy his wife's baking prowess. Even when she did have to leave right away, Dorcas Atkins always insisted on giving her a cake or loaf of homemade bread or some other deliciousness to take to the clinic. No doubt, Polly was sitting at the receptionist desk this very moment drooling over whatever baked goodies Harriet would bring back with her.

Mrs. Atkins did not disappoint. She had an uncanny knack for knowing exactly when her husband would return from the pasture. Harriet had barely stepped through the door into the brightly lit kitchen when the kettle whistled and an oven timer buzzed.

After a quick greeting and a wash-up, she slid into an antique church pew that served as seating for one side of the handmade oaken table. The pew had come from a small church in a Northumberland village where Mrs. Atkins's family had lived for generations stretching back to the days of the Vikings.

Mrs. Atkins poured the tea while urging Harriet to help herself to a slice of the freshly baked coble cake with a dollop of cream whipped up, she was sure, from the morning's milking. The local specialty resembled the coble boat for which it was named, a traditional flat-bottomed boat with a high bow commonly used by fishermen along the Yorkshire coast.

A gooey apple purée oozed between two sponge layers spiced with ginger, cinnamon, and nutmeg. Harriet sighed with contentment as the tantalizing aromas caused her mouth to water. The sweetness of the apples and the spiciness of the cake mingled with the yumminess of the whipped cream.

Mrs. Atkins wanted an update on the flock and especially her three favorite ewes. Harriet reassured her that all the ewes were in great health and ready to become mamas again.

The conversation turned to local matters, such as a neighbor who was recovering from a long illness and the upcoming White Church Autumn Bazaar.

"Mr. Atkins and I are quite excited about the reopening of the Beacon-on-the-Moor Playhouse," Mrs. Atkins enthused as she added more whipped cream to her plate. "My granddaughter refinished the old dressing tables, and I must declare, I believe she did a fine job. It would have been such a shame to have them tossed away like rubbish when all they needed was a bit of spit, polish, and glue."

"I haven't seen the completed pieces," Harriet said. "The contractors have been working on the backstage area this past week, so hopefully the dressing rooms will be finished soon."

"We plan to be at the grand opening," Mr. Atkins said, patting his wife's hand. "Mrs. Atkins and I went to the Beacon on our very first date. Remember that, luv?"

Mrs. Atkins beamed at her husband. "You don't think I'd ever forget now, do you?" She turned to Harriet. "It was Christmastime, and the local community theater group joined with the schools to put on the most wonderful show. First everyone sang hymns and songs, and then they performed *The Christmas Carol*. I'll never forget the little boy who played Tiny Tim. Such a small fellow, but he sure could deliver his lines."

She frowned. "I don't remember whatever happened to that boy. How old would he be now?"

"Not as old as us," Mr. Atkins teased. "I remember most how the pastor—not Pastor Will, mind you, nor Pastor Cummings before him, since this was nigh on half a century ago. His name was Pastor Singletary, and he had a singular voice, yes he did. A voice like you might hear on the radio. At the end of the play, he got on the stage and recited the second chapter of Luke while the schoolchildren acted out the Nativity story. It was a grand night, especially when I walked my date to her door and kissed her under the mistletoe."

He winked at Mrs. Atkins, whose wrinkled cheeks flushed as if she were a schoolgirl. Harriet smiled and breathed a prayer that she and Will would always enjoy each other's company as much as the Atkinses enjoyed each other.

"It might be fun to do something like that this Christmas," she said. "I wonder if Joel has anything planned for the holidays. Or if there's even enough time for rehearsals."

"I'd think it would be good for him to host something at the playhouse, even if it was nothing more than a community Christmas carol sing-along," Mrs. Atkins replied. "It was such a sad day for us when the theater closed, wasn't it, Mr. Atkins? All that drama."

Something in Mrs. Atkins's tone caught Harriet's attention. If she were a mouse, she was sure her nose would start twitching as if she'd caught the scent of cheese. Except, in her case, she'd caught the scent of something amiss.

"What happened?" she asked.

"This traveling troupe had come to town," Mrs. Atkins said. "I forget where they were from."

She gave her husband a questioning look, but he responded with an exaggerated "don't-ask-me" shrug as he swallowed a huge bite of the coble cake.

"I guess it doesn't matter," Mrs. Atkins continued. "They were performing *Pride and Prejudice*, just as you all are doing. Mr. Atkins got us tickets as a birthday present for me. We didn't get out much in those days, you understand, not with three little ones to tend."

She paused, and Mr. Atkins took up the story, almost as if they'd told it so often over the years that they had their own lines to recite.

"We'd made sure to get good seats, right in the center section. We weren't taking a chance on one of those special upper boxes. Not after the railing broke on one of them."

Mr. Atkins seemed as if he was about to say more, but the landline rang from another room. "I'll go see who's giving us a call while you ladies go on with your visiting," he said. He got up and ambled out of the kitchen.

Mrs. Atkins continued the story. "Miss Fern Chapman came over to stay with the babes, and we were all spiffed up in our Sunday finest. First, we went to a fine dinner at the White Hart and then to the playhouse. Only to find everyone in an uproar and, contrary to what we've all heard, the show was *not* going to go on."

Harriet had heard the story of how the Beacon had unexpectedly closed. When Joel first arrived to reopen the theater, several of the older folk at church had talked about their memories of seeing shows there—just like the Atkinses were doing now—and mentioned the sudden shutting of its doors.

"I heard there was a huge thunderstorm that caused flooding," she said.

Mr. Atkins returned to the table. "Wrong number, that call." He shifted in his seat and folded his hands on the table. "It's sure enough true that storm seemed to come out of nowhere. Knocked out a few power lines and caused flooding in more than one of our local establishments."

"There was no warning at all," Mrs. Atkins murmured.

"We talked about coming straight home after our dinner," Mr. Atkins added, "but the Beacon was only a mile or two out of the way, so we called Fern…"

"She said the kids were fine…"

"And we went to the theater." Mr. Atkins paused to shake his head as if in disbelief.

Disbelief about what? Harriet couldn't imagine, yet her insides tingled with anticipation. Either Mr. Atkins was a master storyteller, or she was about to learn something important. Though it was quite possible both those things were true. She willed herself not to fidget but to patiently wait for the Atkinses to complete their story.

"Others were there too," Mr. Atkins continued. "The women mostly waiting in their cars while the men milled around the front doors. The streetlights were on else we wouldn't have been able to see a thing. But the playhouse was black as pitch. I parked close as I could to the entrance—"

"And I stayed nice and dry in the car. We had the cutest little sports car back then. The most lovely shade of maroon, it was. Believe it or not, I had a purse that almost exactly matched it."

"Oh wow." Harriet managed to sound enthusiastic while tamping down her eagerness for the rest of the story to be told. And beginning to doubt it had an exciting climax. "That must have been stylish."

Mrs. Atkins lifted one shoulder in a girlish gesture that struck Harriet as adorable despite the woman's advanced age. "I thought so at the time, although I suppose it sounds silly now."

"My suit was soaked by the time I got to the door and saw the notice," Mr. Atkins said. "Quite cryptic, it was. 'Performance canceled. Ticket refund information will be forthcoming.' That's how I remember it anyway."

Harriet looked from one to the other, but both of them seemed to have said all they meant to say.

"What happened then?" she finally asked.

"We went home," Mr. Atkins said, as if that was self-explanatory.

"The children were asleep by then," Mrs. Atkins added. "Fern went home, and if I remember right, Mr. Atkins and I stayed up and watched a movie. Can't remember now what it was."

"Hmm." Harriet didn't know what else to say. All her inner tingles had fizzled, as if they'd been caught in that sudden downpour. "I suppose I should be getting back to the clinic. Thank you so much for the coble cake. It was delicious."

"So glad you liked it. I'll wrap up some for you to take to Polly and Pastor Will." Mrs. Atkins rose to bustle around the kitchen.

From experience, Harriet knew better than to argue. Besides, she'd enjoy having another slice of the cake herself. While Mrs. Atkins transferred the cake and whipped cream to plastic containers, Harriet tidied the table. Mr. Atkins said his goodbyes and headed back to his sheep.

The women's companionable silence was broken when Mrs. Atkins released a worried sigh. "I wonder if they ever found that girl."

Harriet's inner tingles fired to life again. "What girl?"

"The one that went missing." A faraway look appeared in Mrs. Atkins's eyes. "Funny. With all the talk we've had about the Beacon lately—even with our granddaughter being hired on to redo the dressing tables—I'd forgotten all about that young girl until this very minute."

"Who was she?" Harriet asked.

"One of the actresses. Only about eighteen or nineteen, I think." Mrs. Atkins's eyes brightened, as if her memory had brought long-forgotten details into focus. "She played the part of Lydia Bennet. That's the wild sister, right? The one who runs away with the wicked soldier?"

"That's right."

"I remember reading somewhere at the time that life had imitated art." Mrs. Atkins placed lids on the two plastic containers and placed them in a canvas bag. "Turns out she'd eloped with another actor. Though not the one playing the soldier. Or maybe she eloped with someone else altogether. I don't rightly remember. For a few days, though, when it seemed she'd simply disappeared, we were all on edge and locking our doors."

"Is that why the performance was canceled? Because she disappeared?"

"The storm knocked out the power, and the theater flooded. I don't think anyone knew then that the actress was gone. In fact, she may not have even left yet." Mrs. Atkins scrunched her nose then let out a deprecating laugh. "It's been so long ago. As important as it all felt at the time, now the specifics aren't much more than a misty memory. But I seem to recall hearing she was with a few of the other actors at the Crow's Nest playing darts before the performance. Somebody, I don't remember who, said she was accosted by a couple of men and after that she was nervous and jumpy."

Harriet found herself intrigued by the strange story of a pretend Lydia Bennet eloping, even if she'd hadn't run off with the pretend

George Wickham. "Do you remember the actress's name?" she asked as she slid into her jacket.

"I doubt I ever knew it. None of the performers were what you'd call 'big-name stars,' though it was fun to see them out and about in the village while they were here. I ran into this particular one a couple of times when I was running errands." Mrs. Atkins hefted the canvas bag by its straps and handed it to Harriet with a glimmer in her eyes. "This is all yours now. You don't even have to share the cake if you don't want."

"Don't tempt me," Harriet joked.

She was almost out the door when Mrs. Atkins spoke again.

"Eugenie," she said.

Harriet turned back. "Excuse me?"

"The actress's name was Eugenie. I remember because Princess Eugenie was born a few years later to Prince Andrew and Fergie. When the palace announced the name, I said to Mr. Atkins, 'That was the name of the actress who caused all that fuss.' Yes," she said firmly. "I'm sure of it. But I can't tell you what her last name was. Not that it'd be the same now, anyway."

Harriet's curiosity compelled her to want to know more about the actress whose life had imitated one aspect of Lydia Bennet's story. Despite her reckless choices and with the help of her family, Lydia had managed to land on her feet. But had Eugenie?

Harriet frowned as she slid into the Beast and started the engine. Her mind whirled with questions as she tried to make sense of what she'd learned.

If Eugenie had been with other troupe members at the Crow's Nest, then she must have intended to perform that Friday night. Who were the two men who "accosted" her? What did they want, and what had they said that made her nervous? Did they threaten her?

Had she truly eloped?

There had to be more to the story, and Harriet's natural curiosity—like an itch she needed to scratch—wouldn't let her rest until she found out those unknown details.

A shiver of foreboding chilled Harriet to the bone as an unexpected thought occurred to her. Could the elopement story be a cover-up for an entirely different turn of events? Perhaps something unexpected had happened to Eugenie.

Perhaps something sinister.

CHAPTER FIVE

As soon as Harriet pulled out of the lane leading from the Atkinses' farm, she called Joel's number. Not that she expected him to answer. The director often seemed to be without his phone. During rehearsals, he kept it locked in a drawer in his office so, in his words, "It neither interrupts me nor distracts me." On the few occasions she and Will had joined him for a bite out, Joel somehow worked it into the conversation that he'd left his phone at home or in his car.

Harriet couldn't decide if the habit, which seemed odd for someone so driven to get the theater's building and its production up-and-running, was an eccentricity or an affectation. Wouldn't he want to be tethered to his phone so he didn't miss an important message? After last night's heartfelt confession, she wanted to give him the benefit of the doubt. But she couldn't stop wondering if he was avoiding phone calls or texts.

When her call went to voice mail, she left a brief message. "I heard an interesting story about an actress who went missing when the theater closed. Have you heard anything about that? Call me if you get a chance. Otherwise, I'll see you this evening."

She ended the call while slowing to maneuver a curve on the narrow road. "He's not going to call me back," she murmured. Though surely anyone around there who was at least sixty knew the story.

Mrs. Atkins even said everyone had been on edge until they learned about the actress's elopement. It only made sense that at least one person would have told Joel about the mystery.

She could always ask Aunt Jinny about it. She'd have been—Harriet did a rough calculation in her head—in her twenties when the theater closed. And away at university or medical school at the time. So even if her parents had talked about such mysterious news, Aunt Jinny may not have been there during the excitement and the gossip. A young woman devoted to her studies and maybe even being courted about that same time probably didn't give much thought to hometown gossip.

Harriet dropped that idea and replayed the conversation with the Atkinses in a vain attempt to pinpoint what bothered her about the story. Why was she so suspicious that Occam's Razor, the investigative philosophy that the simplest explanation is usually the right explanation, didn't apply to Eugenie's disappearance?

Maybe Harriet had read too many mysteries and seen too many crime shows.

"There's no mystery here." Though her only audience was the colorful parrot-shaped air freshener that Will had hung from her rearview mirror, she said the words out loud. As if saying *and* hearing them made them truer.

But her inner tingles, now clumped together in the pit of her stomach, refused to fade away. Even Lydia, as young and silly as she was, had left a note for her friend. Wouldn't Eugenie have done the same?

"There's at least a bit of a mystery," Harriet said to the colorful parrot. "Apparently no one in the troupe knew of the elopement when Eugenie went missing. How did they find out about it?"

On a whim, at the next crossroads, she turned toward Whitby, the nearest large town, instead of taking the road to Cobble Hill Farm. She didn't need to be back at the clinic until two. Why not do a little sleuthing on her own? Maybe she could at least find out the answer to her "bit of a mystery."

Fifteen minutes later, she entered the *Whitby Gazette* newspaper office. She greeted Colleen Carruthers, the good-natured redhead who worked the front desk. After writing a bestselling novel, which critics considered a literary masterpiece, Colleen ticked that item off her bucket list and never wrote for publication again. She used her generous royalties to purchase a fifty-acre run-down farm, modernize the cottage and outbuildings, and obtain foundation stock so she could raise Shetland ponies, Shetland cattle, and Shetland sheepdogs.

The *Gazette* position, where she oversaw advertising sales while also performing routine office duties, had allowed her to meet local business owners, civic leaders, and community movers and shakers when she first moved to the area several years ago. She also had access to the vast majority of the local news—that which was printed and, more importantly, that which wasn't. All that, along with her engaging personality, meant that she quickly became a popular individual in the town.

"I'm here to do some research in the archives," Harriet said after the women exchanged the usual pleasantries. "Is the computer room available?"

"No one's been in all day. All you need to do is sign in." Colleen gestured to the open logbook on the counter. "What are you researching this time?"

Harriet shared the story about the missing actress as she wrote the date and her name on the appropriate line in the logbook. "Her first name is Eugenie, but I don't know her last name."

"Okehurst," Colleen replied. "You're talking about Eugenie Okehurst. Though your Mrs. Atkins is mistaken on one point. Eugenie played Elizabeth, not Lydia. There was a mistake on the early promotional materials, so it's no wonder she was confused."

Harriet's eyes widened so much while Colleen spoke that they ached. "I can't believe you know about her."

"Knowing things is my hobby. Besides, I'm always interested in what's going on in our little corner of England. When I heard about the theater reopening, I did a little research on the who, what, when, where, and why of its closing. The downside of the *Gazette* being a weekly is that only two articles were printed about Ms. Okehurst's 'mysterious disappearance.'" Colleen rolled her eyes as she made the air quotes. "One when she went missing, and the other saying she was safe and sound in Scotland. Which, if I do say so myself, is a nice place to be safe and sound. I lived there for a time and can speak from personal experience."

Colleen, who always had an anecdote to add to any conversation, could say she'd once lived on the moon and Harriet would almost believe it. She chose not to comment on Colleen's time in Scotland and, instead, frowned in disappointment.

"Only two articles? At least they won't be hard to find again now that I know what name to search."

"Easier than you think." Colleen tapped the keys on her computer and, a moment later, the nearby printer whirred to life. "I saved them in a folder along with a few articles on the play itself. You know the kind of thing—how excited everyone was to go see it, a fawning critique from the opening matinee."

She straightened the pages that emerged from the printer then slid them into an envelope. "Here you go."

"I can't thank you enough for these," Harriet said, taking the envelope from her.

"Glad to be of help. Though, if you don't mind me asking, why are you so interested in a mystery that's already been solved?"

Because it might not have been.

As much as Harriet liked Colleen, she didn't want to admit her doubt in the established story. Though Colleen was known as someone who could keep a secret, an admirable trait considering her position, Harriet's unfounded suspicion hardly counted as classified material. How embarrassing if news raced around town that she was investigating a cold case that might have been closed when it was still hot. Nope! Not going to take that risk.

Fortunately, she had a second reason. Not a great one, but it might work.

"Turns out I have more of a reason than I knew. I'm playing Elizabeth Bennet." Harriet smiled. "It sounds silly, I suppose, but even when I thought Eugenie played Lydia, I felt a connection with her. I'd like to write her if I could find her address. Or send an email."

Colleen's eyes sparkled. "Wouldn't it be exciting if she came to a performance?"

Stunned by the suggestion, Harriet actually took a step backward.

"But we're amateurs." Her voice squeaked the words. She couldn't bear the thought of a professional actress judging her performance of Jane Austen's most beloved character. "It would be awful to have her in the audience. I think I'd faint." As soon as the words were out of her mouth, she laughed at how melodramatic she sounded.

Colleen laughed with her. "All I'm saying is, if you find her, send her an invite. Though I wish you luck with that. I'm known for my online sleuthing skills, and I scoured the internet. Despite my best efforts, I couldn't find any information on her after she eloped. Knowing her married name would have helped, but even so, it's odd there's no mention of her."

"You found nothing?"

"The poor girl didn't even rate an entry in Wikipedia. It's like she completely disappeared."

Colleen's words, spoken so lightly, landed heavy as a stone in Harriet's heart.

Perhaps that's because she did.

Settled at a corner table in the local diner, Harriet ordered an autumn harvest salad with an apple cider vinaigrette and a cup of cinnamon tea. Once the waitress was gone, she opened the envelope Colleen had given her. The first page showed an advertisement for the play, starring Eugenie Okehurst as the inimitable Elizabeth Bennet, with the show dates and ticket prices. The page was followed by a few printed articles arranged in chronological order.

Harriet skipped past the ones touting the upcoming show and the promotional pieces on the cast members, intending to read them later, and focused on the two that mattered to her most.

The headline on the first article read: ACTRESS DISAPPEARS: WHAT HAPPENED TO ELIZABETH?

> Eugenie Okehurst, the latest darling of the London theater circuit, went missing during the recent thunderstorm that caused the cancellation of Saturday night's performance of Pride and Prejudice at the Beacon-on-the-Moor Playhouse.
>
> Because the show was cancelled, Ms. Okehurst's absence wasn't noticed until the following afternoon when she didn't appear at a charity tea hosted by the local chapter of the Yorkshire Literary Society.
>
> Ms. Okehurst, who is only eighteen years old, and her leading man, Roland Tate, who plays the role of Fitzwilliam Darcy in the play, were scheduled to participate in a skit with students from the Cliffside Academy Drama Club at the event.
>
> The subsequent search included a visit to Sea-Holly Cottage, where Ms. Okehurst was staying with Juliana Channing and Verity Stapleton, the actresses playing, respectively, Jane Bennet and Charlotte Lucas. During questioning, both actresses stated they believed Ms. Okehurst had taken shelter in town, since portions of the road to the cottage were underwater from the heavy downpour. They stated to this reporter that they contacted the police after Mr. Tate called to ask about Ms. Okehurst's whereabouts.
>
> "All her clothes are still here," Ms. Channing said to this reporter. "Even her glasses and her contact lens case. It's like she vanished into the night. I just know something awful has happened to her, or she would have called us."

"Strange," Harriet murmured to herself. To the best of her knowledge, disposable contacts weren't available in the 1980s. Her mom had mentioned something a time or two about sterilizing her rigid contact lenses in a special solution at least seven or eight hours a night. That was why, as a younger woman, she always had a pair of prescription glasses too. How strange that Eugenie had left those things behind. Plus, wouldn't she have taken at least one change of clothes?

The lengthy article, dated October 16, 1985, accompanied by a publicity photograph of the young actress, went on to describe how radio broadcasts and the local news stations asked their audiences to call a special hotline number if they had any information on Ms. Okehurst's whereabouts. As Mrs. Atkins had said, Eugenie had been with other troupe members at the Crow's Nest, but none of them seemed to know when she'd left or where she'd gone. Despite their best efforts, the investigators received no credible leads, and possible sightings of the actress were proven false. Teams of volunteers searched the surrounding countryside to no avail.

The final paragraphs of the story detailed how the storm's ferocity caused enough damage to the theater that the next weekend's performances, the last ones of the play's run, had to be canceled. As the individual cast and crew members were cleared from any involvement in Eugenie's disappearance, they were given permission to leave White Church Bay, although they were warned they might be recalled to the village for future questioning.

The reporter, whose name Harriet didn't recognize, pleaded with her readers to never give up their search for the missing actress and to report anything suspicious—no matter how inconsequential the incident—to the police. The community was warned to be wary of strangers and to lock their doors at night.

"Excuse me, ma'am." The waitress stood beside the table with Harriet's salad and tea.

Though startled by the unexpected interruption, Harriet smiled and moved the papers out of the way. Despite her eagerness to return to the article, she took a deep calming breath, prepared her tea, and dressed her salad. The first bite of mixed greens with a slice of roasted carrot tasted exactly like autumn should.

She took a few more bites then returned to the article's closing—an impassioned, though perhaps over-the-top, warning.

> *When an esteemed visitor to our village is snatched away, never to be seen again, we must rise as one to seek justice for the lost and prove ourselves as friends indeed to our neighbors who are in need.*

"That sounds like something Mary Bennet might say," Harriet murmured to herself. Then she continued reading.

> *The moral rot that has seized hold of our cities, allowing criminal behavior to fester and grow, has stretched its hand toward our moors, seeking to ensnare our communities in its evil grip. This hand must be slapped, with ferocity and immediacy, to ensure our future tranquility and serenity.*

"Wow." Harriet blew out an amused breath at the overwrought emotion expressed by the sensationalist reporter. Nancy Lennox definitely had her own signature style—one that went well beyond the requisite Ws of journalism. It was almost nostalgic in its lack of objectivity.

Except the article had been written about a young woman who'd gone missing with no clue as to where she'd gone. There was nothing amusing or nostalgic about that.

While enjoying her salad, Harriet turned to the next printed page, an article written one week later by the same reporter. The headline, in even bigger font than the one before, declared: ACTRESS FOUND! MARRIAGE BELLS RING!

> *In a plot twist no one saw coming, it's now known that Eugenie Okehurst is alive and well after abandoning the fame of the theater for the delights of domesticity. Ms. Okehurst, it seems, was miscast when she took on the role of the sensible Elizabeth Bennet in the recent production of Jane Austen's* Pride and Prejudice *being performed at the Beacon-on-the-Moor Playhouse before a brutal storm caused damage to the theatre and ended the show's run.*
>
> *Ms. Okehurst should have instead been given the role of the foolhardy Lydia Bennet so that her recent escapade could be more fittingly described as an example of life imitating art.*
>
> *Investigators now know that Ms. Okehurst and an unidentified man traveled to Gretna Green, where they participated in a ceremony not unlike thousands, nay, hundreds of thousands, before them, including the fictional George and Lydia Wickham.*

Another actress in the cast, whose identity is being withheld by the lead investigator in the missing persons case out of privacy concerns, received a note written by Ms. Okehurst, expressing her joy in her new life and her regret at causing such an unexpected ruckus.

Our community can now take a collective sigh of relief at the knowledge that no untoward shenanigans took place in our North Sea paradise. Indeed, we can take pride in how we rallied together in our deep concern for a gallivanting stranger, how we searched our moors in vain, and how we now demonstrate compassion and forgiveness to one who, it might be said, behaved without thought of consequences.

A prosperous and happy future is wished for Ms. Okehurst and her anonymous groom.

"Ohh-kay," Harriet said aloud, drawing out the word while skimming through the articles again.

Her suspicions about this being an unsolved mystery might have been eased except for all the anonymity. Who received Eugenie's letter? Who was the groom? Why not report their names? It didn't make any sense, especially when the groom's name must have been a matter of public record. Which meant Nancy Lennox should have been able to find it. Did she even try?

No matter. Harriet would give it a go. Immediately, her stomach tightened.

Colleen, with all her internet skills and access to databases, hadn't been able to discover Eugenie's married name. How could Harriet hope to succeed where Colleen had failed?

As Harriet returned the pages to the envelope, another thought struck her. If Eugenie's groom was a local or a member of the troupe, had his absence set off any alarm bells? Had anyone missed him?

She glanced at her watch. If she hurried, she could stop at the police station in White Church Bay before returning to the clinic for her afternoon appointments. Eugenie's missing person's report should be public record. If it was, Harriet could get a copy and find out if anyone else had gone missing from the area around the same time.

The door of the diner flew open, and two men, both wearing suits and appearing to be in their midfifties, strolled in.

"Hello, darlin'," one of them boomed to the hostess. He ignored the PLEASE WAIT TO BE SEATED sign and strutted to a table in the center of the dining area with his companion following in his wake. They took their seats and gazed around the room as if they owned the place.

For all Harriet knew, maybe they did. She focused on finishing her salad, intent on not making eye contact.

The hostess, a graying brunette with a matronly figure, straightened her jacket and approached the table with the menus.

"We don't need those," the loud-mouthed man said. "I come here every Friday, and I get the same meal every Friday. That's not gonna change. You already know what I want."

"All right, Mr. Dankworth. Would you like a basket of freshly baked rolls today?"

"You ask me that question every week, darlin'. It makes no sense to me, but that's what you do."

Harriet refrained from glancing at the table, but it wasn't easy. What an incredibly rude and condescending man. She mentally searched for his name among those she'd heard since moving to Yorkshire but couldn't recall ever hearing it before. As unusual as it was, she was sure she'd remember if she had.

"I need to ask, Mr. Dankworth," the hostess said, her tone deferential yet firm. "Sometimes you say yes, and sometimes you say no. It's always a guessing game with you when it comes to the bread basket."

Good for you! Harriet inwardly cheered. She sensed that the "darlin's" graciousness to the overbearing Dankworth would only go so far.

A loud guffaw broke the overlong silence. "True, true," Dankworth admitted. "Today is a yes."

"I'll be right back."

Once the hostess left, Dankworth kept talking, apparently carrying on a conversation he and his companion were having before they entered the diner.

"There's only room for one," he said. "We don't need some upstart from who knows where coming into this area with his fancy plans."

Harriet froze as the other man murmured something in a voice too low for her to hear.

"You should have heard my great-uncle Egbert when he found out. 'Ruined that place once, and I'll do it again.' That's what he said. As if he can even leave the estate these days."

Once again, the other man spoke too softly for Harriet to hear his response.

"Who knows what he meant by it?" Dankworth spouted. "No more competition, and that's the point. Great-uncle Egbert didn't like competition then, and I don't like it now. But enough of all that. We've got other business to discuss."

Harriet glanced at her watch again. As much as she wanted to stick around to hear more, she needed to get going. She gathered her things and headed for the register to pay her check.

As she left the diner, clutching her bag and the envelope, Dankworth's words played over again in her mind. *We don't need some upstart from who knows where coming into this area with his fancy plans.* Was he talking about Joel?

Had she just met the man who'd sent the threatening notes?

CHAPTER SIX

More determined than ever to stop at the police station after what she'd heard in the Whitby diner, Harriet drove toward White Church Bay. Along the way, she called Will and told him what the Dankworth fellow had said.

"Give me a minute," Will said. "I'm looking up the name."

"He could have been talking about the Beacon."

"He may have been," Will agreed. "Cyril A. Dankworth is the CEO of Dankworth Enterprises, which owns and operates the Whitby Majestic."

Harriet's heart dropped. "The theater we go to?"

"That's the one."

"Ugh. I'll never be able to go there again."

Will chuckled. "Sometimes ignorance is bliss. Though not in this situation."

"What I don't understand," Harriet said, "is why he considers the Beacon, which will have live performances, as competition to his movie theater."

"The Beacon can do both, since it also has a screen. Though maybe it's simply a matter of where people spend their entertainment dollars. Whatever Dankworth's reasoning, I need to call Joel and tell him about this."

"And I'll tell Van." Harriet slowed the Beast to maneuver a hedge-lined curve. "I'm on my way to the police station to look up Eugenie's missing person's report. I'll be there in a few minutes."

"Who's Eugenie?" Will's tone mingled concern with bewilderment.

"An old mystery I stumbled upon. I'll tell you all about it later."

"Can't wait to hear it. For now," Will cautioned, "though I agree Van should know about Dankworth, that's Joel's decision to make. Not ours. I doubt he's even told Van about the notes."

Harriet frowned. Despite their urging last night, Joel didn't seem gung ho on talking to Van. And, of course, Will was right, but she really wanted to spill out the entire conversation to Van. But if Will didn't want her to tell Van, then she probably shouldn't tell Polly either. Maybe she could call Aunt Jinny later and spill all the tea with her.

"This isn't going to be easy," she said. "Keeping news like this to myself."

"I know." Will's sympathetic tone was laced with humor. "But I'm confident you'll manage, and I love you."

"I love you too."

She ended the call as she pulled into the parking lot located on top of one of the two bluffs that stood on either side of the quaint village. The view from the top never failed to stir a sense of contented wonder within Harriet's heart.

She stepped out of the Beast and gazed across to the opposite side. White Church, where Will served as pastor, had overlooked the bay from atop that bluff since the early years of the eighteenth century. From where she stood, Harriet could see the windswept gravestones huddled near the church's whitewashed walls.

Though historians dated White Church Bay to the early 1500s, its origins stretched back to the days of the Vikings who settled in the area about a thousand years after Jesus's birth. Between the bluffs, the oldest shops and homes lined a maze of narrow streets and alleyways along the steep decline to the rocky shores of the North Sea. The access to this historic section of the village, which descended to the shore, was limited to foot traffic and the occasional motorized carts or emergency vehicles.

Harriet couldn't count the number of times she'd walked down the steep stairs on her way to the library, the bank, or her favorite shops. Like the locals, she knew not to purchase more than she could carry back up those stairs unless she'd brought a wheeled tote of some kind with her.

She wouldn't trade such minor—okay, sometimes they were major—inconveniences to live anywhere else in the world. Sure, she missed her family and the friends she'd left behind in Connecticut. But this little spot in God's creation with its North Sea wind and waves, wild and untamed moors, and deep-rooted history and traditions connected her heart to her paternal ancestors.

With a prayer of gratitude for all God's blessings, Harriet adjusted the strap of her bag over her shoulder and passed Van's cruiser as she headed for the squat building that housed the police station.

Van had been among the first locals to welcome Harriet to the community when she arrived to claim her inheritance and take over Grandad's veterinary clinic. The eighteen or so months between then and now had flown by—and brought with them significant changes.

Harriet had arrived in Yorkshire after a broken engagement, and now she was married to Will and couldn't imagine her life without him.

And then there was Van. The detective constable had finally captured the heart of the woman he'd crushed on seemingly forever. After helping Harriet solve a mystery involving Nazi art theft during World War II about four months ago, he and Polly had announced their impromptu elopement in a text message.

From Gretna Green.

Just like Eugenie Okehurst and her anonymous groom.

That didn't help answer any of Harriet's questions, but hopefully she could find answers in the police records. And Van could help. She only needed to shove aside any thoughts about the scene from the Whitby Diner until she was alone again.

She entered the constabulary office to find Van at one of the wooden desks on the other side of the front counter. He held a phone cradled to his ear and was taking notes on a pad.

He looked up and smiled at her. "One minute," he mouthed.

Harriet wasn't surprised that no one else was in the office, since the administrative clerk only worked part-time. Though there were often petty crimes to be solved in the community, serious wrongdoing was minimal. On the rare times a stronger police presence was needed, the officers from nearby Whitby were on hand to help out.

Most of the time, though, Van handled everything from traffic infractions and accidents to the occasional shoplifting charge.

After ending his call, Van approached the counter and greeted Harriet. "I didn't expect to see you until rehearsal this evening," he said. "I've memorized almost all my lines, but it's easier to say them at the kitchen table with Polly than on stage in front of a crowd."

"You'll do great," Harriet said, smiling. Though she wouldn't say so to Van, or even to Polly, she thought his occasional mishaps during rehearsals made him an even more believable Mr. Bingley. He definitely had the same wide-eyed eagerness and kindly demeanor as his character. Plus, he didn't have to act at pretending to be in love with Jane. He was as besotted with Polly, and she with him, as the characters they played were with each other.

"I admit, I'm nervous too," she said. "Since we're all amateurs, I imagine our audience will be gracious."

"I hope you're right about that. Our main concern right now should be opening night. Whether or not it has to be delayed."

Harriet narrowed her eyes. "Why would it be delayed?"

"Isn't that why you're here? To talk about the mysteries of the theater?" He lifted his hands as if warding off danger, pretending to be afraid.

"You know about Kezia's ghost." It wasn't a question. She'd expected Polly would tell her husband what Harriet had told her. "I wish I knew what she really saw."

Van bent forward and folded his arms on the counter. "This is about more than a ghost. Apparently, other strange things have been happening there, such as unexplained noises and sudden cold chills. All the typical haunted theater stuff."

"I haven't heard anything about that." Odd that Joel hadn't mentioned such instances at dinner last night. He'd only shown her and Will his latest threatening note.

"From what I understand, a few of the cast members went to the Crow's Nest after rehearsal yesterday," Van replied. "One or two had called Kezia to be sure she was all right, but she didn't want to talk to anyone."

He straightened and beat out a quick rhythm on the counter. "Then that gal who plays Kitty—or maybe she plays Mary—I'm always getting those two mixed up—she starts talking about these unexplained noises, and a few others admit to feeling these strange blasts of cold air. Seems like every one of them had a story."

Harriet hardly knew what to think. She wouldn't have thought anyone in the cast would be susceptible to such nonsense. If such things were actually happening, there had to be a legitimate reason. Perhaps something was wrong with the ventilation ducts.

"Nothing like that has happened to me."

A huge grin spread across Van's boyish face. "You sound disappointed."

"I guess I am. If I'd experienced something strange, maybe I could figure out what was really going on."

"That old building's been abandoned for decades," Van said. "When I was a kid, we used to dare one another to go into it. Being rambunctious blokes, we secretly wanted it to be haunted. Unfortunately for us, there was nothing inside but old furnishings and trash. Though I suppose that was a good thing."

He flashed another grin. "Maybe all that reconstruction work woke up a ghost."

Harriet rolled her eyes at him and laughed. "There has to be a logical explanation for whatever Kezia saw."

"I talked to Joel this morning and offered to take a look around. He said not to bother. But if you think I should, I can poke around a little during rehearsal tonight."

Harriet considered Van's proposal. She could poke around too, when she wasn't needed on stage. But considering what Will had said about Joel needing to make the decision about if and when to bring in the police, it didn't seem fair to give Van her go-ahead after Joel had refused Van's offer.

"That's up to you," she finally said, deciding it wasn't her place to make a decision for him either. "Like I said, I didn't know anything about all these other incidents. I stopped in to talk about a different mystery. Though in a way, it's related, since it has to do with the theater."

"I'm all ears."

Harriet told Van what she'd learned from the Atkinses then showed him the articles she'd gotten from the *Gazette*. "Have you ever heard anything about this? Maybe from retired officers talking about strange cases they investigated? Something like that?"

"Not that I remember. Think about it though. Even a twenty-something officer back then would be in his sixties now and probably retired. They'd be under the twenty-five years of service scheme." Van moved to a computer station located at one end of the counter. "Let me see if I can find something in the records database."

"From that long ago?"

"Cross your fingers." Van opened the program he wanted and placed the cursor in the search bar. "Tell me that name again. Last name, then first name."

"Okehurst, Eugenie."

"That's O-A-K—"

"It's O-K-E," Harriet said, correcting him. "H-U-R-S-T."

"Got it. First name?"

Harriet spelled out *Eugenie* for him, then he clicked the enter button. The database responded with one result that included a hyperlinked case number.

"I'm surprised the database goes back forty years," Harriet said as Van clicked the link.

"You can thank our turn-of-the-century Parliament," Van said. "They funded a modernization initiative to computerize older records."

The uploaded page provided little information beyond the basics. The category, *Missing Persons*, was given along with Eugenie's name, date of birth, and physical description. The only log note referenced the number for the evidence file.

"That file should be in storage." Van wrinkled his nose. "In the vault."

Even though she knew what he was going to say before he said it, Harriet released a groan. The vault was the euphemistic name for the damp, mildewy basement. She'd heard stories about the place from Van. And it wasn't a place she was eager to visit.

The underground rooms had been constructed at least fifty years ago, maybe a hundred years ago, in an already existing cavern. The entire cliff was a network of caves and tunnels that eventually led to the sea. If only those rocky walls could talk, the tales they could tell of smuggling operations, kidnappings, and who knew what other nefarious schemes.

"You can stay here while I brave the horrors of the vault," Van said. "Since the investigation only lasted a few days, there probably won't be much except the original case notes. Maybe the volunteer sign-up pages, though I don't know if they required those back then.

All to say, I'd be surprised if there's much more in the box than a couple of folders."

"I'm happy to wait for you." Harriet glanced at the clock and grimaced. "Though not for too long. I have to head to the clinic pretty soon."

"I'll be quick."

As Van disappeared through a rear door, Harriet checked her phone. No texts or calls from Polly—that was good news. Nothing from Will, either, but that wasn't surprising. He probably hadn't been able to reach Joel.

Besides, Will had his own full calendar today and needed to finish his appointments so he wouldn't be late for this evening's rehearsal. Thankfully, they didn't have to worry about supper. Joel had arranged for Seadog Street Deli to cater sandwiches, salads, and drinks for the cast and crew.

When Van returned, he carried a dilapidated cardboard box to his desk and removed the lid. "I warned you there wouldn't be much," he said as he placed a thin folder on the counter. "That's the case report with the investigative records. But here's the prize."

He placed a second folder on top of the first and opened it to reveal a handwritten letter. "The note from Eugenie."

Harriet gasped. Unable to take her eyes from the faded yellow paper, she asked, "Can I read it?"

"I'll make you a copy of it and the police interview." Though the letter wasn't sealed in an evidence bag, Van put on a pair of latex gloves before handling it. "I wish we had the envelope too, but it's not here."

"Without the envelope, we can't know where the letter came from."

"Except that Eugenie specifically mentions Gretna Green," Van said as he made the copies. "Though I guess the letter didn't have to be mailed from there. We have no idea where Eugenie and her new husband went after their wedding or how long afterward she wrote it."

Harriet glanced at the clock again as Van handed her the copies. "I'm going to be late if I don't leave this minute," she said, placing the sheets of paper in the envelope with her documents from the *Gazette*. "I'll have to read through these later. Oh, I almost forgot. Could you see if any local men went missing around the same time?"

"You mean Eugenie's groom? I've got a few things to finish up, but as soon as I get a chance, I'll check," Van said as Harriet headed for the door. "I'll also look through the Okehurst investigative reports. Maybe I'll find something helpful, though I'm not sure what you're trying to find."

With her hand on the doorknob, she turned back to him. "All I want is positive proof that Eugenie went to Gretna Green. That she actually got married."

"Why do you think she didn't?"

Harriet pressed her lips together, knowing she needed to give Van a reasonable answer but not yet wanting to share what Mrs. Atkins had told her about the men Eugenie had an encounter with. "I guess I don't like loose threads," she finally said. "And this note, supposedly sent *after* the wedding, seems to be a little too convenient for my liking."

Van chuckled. "You could be right. But I'm more concerned about what might be going on at the Beacon now than I am with what happened over forty years ago."

Though he didn't mean it as a rebuke, Harriet felt a twinge of guilt. She was spending way too much time on a mystery of her own making. Instead of driving to Whitby during her lunch break, she should have taken that time to visit Kezia right here in White Church Bay. That would have been the kind and neighborly thing to do.

Now she wouldn't have a chance to talk to Kezia until rehearsal this evening. And maybe not even then, at least not in private, with so many other people around.

On her way to the Beast, Harriet paused and looked once again over the village rooftops that sloped toward the shore. One of those pitched rooftops belonged to the discount antique store that Kezia and Andrew owned.

The two-story sandstone building, located between a pharmacy and a narrow alley, maintained its natural coloring except for the eaves, the door, and the frames around the two large display windows. Those were painted an eye-pleasing shade of cobalt blue.

In the early years of their marriage, the couple had lived in the shop's upper-level apartment. But they had moved to a more modern home on the bluff a few years before Harriet arrived in Yorkshire. Nowadays Andrew, who served on a renaissance fair organizational committee, used the apartment to store an assortment of medieval costumes and props.

Kezia might be at the store right now. Unfortunately, Harriet was out of time.

It was a strange irony, Harriet mused as she slid into the Beast's driver's seat. A little over a year ago, she'd suspected Andrew of masquerading as the ghost of one of King Arthur's knights. And now the very practical, sensible Kezia claimed to have seen a ghost.

The knight ghost had turned out to be a living, breathing, red-blooded person.

Unless Kezia had been hallucinating—not likely!—her ghost was also a living, breathing, red-blooded person. An imposter who wanted to cause trouble.

Was this new ghost someone's idea of a joke? Or did that someone intend harm to a member of the cast or crew?

Either way, the imposter-ghost needed to be unmasked. Immediately.

CHAPTER SEVEN

Almost as soon as the casting decisions were made, Harriet had learned that one of Joel's major obstacles, as the director of an amateur play, was planning rehearsals around a myriad of work schedules. His solution was to "chunk together" as much as possible scenes that involved the same characters.

Will hadn't needed to come to the rehearsals where Harriet mostly interacted with Mr. Collins and Lady Catherine de Bourgh, and her presence hadn't been required for the scenes between Mr. Darcy and Mr. Bingley's family.

Joel's plan wasn't foolproof, but the cast members did their best to attend as many of their assigned rehearsals as they could. Full-cast rehearsals took place on Friday evenings and on Saturday or Sunday afternoons.

Since Harriet hoped for an opportunity to talk privately with Kezia, she and Will were among the first to arrive at the Beacon. While Will chatted with Joel near the concessions stand where Seadog Street Deli was preparing supper for the cast and crew, Harriet wandered past the box office and theater offices to the south foyer.

The oversized double doors stood wide open, as if inviting her to enter the dimly lit auditorium. She paused when she was about halfway down the aisle to scan the area. Eight rows of four seats each stood between the main aisles and the walls. The middle section consisted of eight rows with a decreasing number of seats the closer one moved toward the stage. Four theater boxes were situated on the upper level, but they were off-limits for now. The theater had to meet a specific income threshold before Joel tackled those renovations.

Harriet slid into a newly cushioned end seat and studied the stage, which was furnished as the Bennet sitting room for the opening scene.

That chair is mine, and the one next to it is Jane's. I'll deliver the well-known opening lines to the audience, take my seat, and pretend to be surprised when Mama rushes in from stage left with the incredible news that a gentleman has leased the estate of Netherfield. A gentleman with four or five thousand pounds a year. Quite the catch indeed for one of her daughters.

Harriet closed her eyes and tried to imagine Eugenie Okehurst in the role. The actress was almost half Harriet's age and lovely with her expressive eyes and high cheekbones. The reporter who wrote the opening performance critique had been effusive in his praise of Eugenie's Elizabeth.

Wonder what he'd think of mine?

Harriet shook away the thought to stop the comparison trap from springing into action. She didn't need to get caught in its ugly jaws, especially when any comparison between a young professional and a thirtysomething amateur wasn't fair. She was determined to take all of Joel's notes and advice to heart, give the best performance possible, and enjoy the once-in-a-lifetime experience.

Because she definitely wouldn't be doing anything like this again.

Amused by the direction her thoughts had taken her, Harriet stood, stretching her aching muscles as she did so. The day had been a long one, starting early in the morning with the sheep examinations at several farms, the trip to Whitby, and her visit with Van, followed by a hectic afternoon at the clinic. She hadn't even taken a moment to read Eugenie's letter, since she didn't want to rush through the experience.

As she started back up the aisle to return to the lobby, she heard a sound like an iconic ghost in a movie. With her senses on high alert, she steadied herself as her eyes darted around the auditorium. The ghostly noise rose and fell, seeming to come from everywhere and yet nowhere at the same time.

Harriet scanned the theater boxes and the shadowy corners for any sign of movement, but she appeared to be alone in the theater. Even if she called for Will, he probably wouldn't hear her. Not if he was still with Joel near the concession stand.

"Who's there?" she called.

"Only me."

Harriet inhaled a sharp breath as she twirled around. A tall figure in dark robes moved among the shadows near the front exit door. "Did I frighten you?" The cultured voice spoke in an unhurried tone as if pleased by Harriet's reaction. "I certainly mean you no harm."

Odette Jones emerged from the shadow into the dim lighting along the front of the stage. She was clad in a black caftan robe with flowing sleeves over a dark gray sweater and black yoga pants and no longer seemed nearly as tall nor as thin. The white swath in her black hair flowed like a ribbon of snow through the ebony mass piled on top of her head.

As she came closer, amusement shone in the shrewd brown eyes framed by heavily penciled eyebrows. A rose powder blushed her lined cheeks while a complementary shade brightened her full lips. The total effect was that of an accomplished older woman with a confident sense of style.

"I say, Dr. Bailey," she continued, stopping a few feet away and resting her hand on the back of the nearest seat, "you're as pale as a pearl in a newly opened oyster. Surely, a woman with your sensibilities didn't see a ghost. Though I've been hearing whispers that this aged theatrical marvel could be haunted."

Harriet gulped a much-needed breath and willed her body to relax. She spoke as casually as she could, considering her heart still raced as if she were being chased by Frankenstein's monster. "You startled me, that's all. I heard a noise, at least I thought I did, just before I saw you."

Odette smiled, her lips pressed together, a smile as enigmatic as the Mona Lisa's. A snatch of dialogue between Elizabeth and her father popped into Harriet's mind.

"*Are you not diverted, Lizzy?*" Mr. Bennet asks his daughter.

"*I am most excessively diverted,*" Elizabeth replies.

Odette, the production's head costume designer, was obviously *diverted*, excessively so, by Harriet's reaction to her unexpected appearance in the auditorium.

"What did you hear?" Odette waved her bronze-colored hand in a dramatic gesture toward the stage. "The echoes of long-ago voices reciting their memorized lines?"

Her arm, enveloped in the black flowing sleeve, swept above the empty seats. "Or perhaps the echoes of laughter from the audience. Comedy. The plaintive sobs of their weeping. Tragedy."

Mesmerized by what could only be described as a performance, Harriet didn't answer until Odette's eyes pierced through her haze.

"I'm sure it wasn't anything more than my overactive imagination." Except...

Someone could be playing tricks. And if that was the case, she was determined to discover who.

"You are well-liked in this community." Odette's spectral Mona Lisa persona faded as a genuine smile softened her steady gaze. "But I suppose you know that."

Harriet's cheeks warmed at the unexpected praise. "I hope that's true," she said. "White Church Bay is my home now."

"I've been told you have a knack for solving mysteries. Finding lost items, unpuzzling puzzles, revealing what is hidden."

"It's true, I've had a few adventures. Mostly I just want to help my friends and neighbors whenever I can." Now that her heartbeat was back to normal, Harriet's voice was stronger. Odette's change in demeanor also helped lessen Harriet's feeling of being off-kilter.

Odette had temporarily moved to the village to oversee the *Pride and Prejudice* costumes. Harriet first met her at a meeting with the other female cast members where Odette had talked about women's fashions in the early 1800s. She'd also displayed a few gowns from her own collection that were suitable for the play. Harriet got the impression that Odette operated a small business providing historic costumes to theaters and small-scale productions.

That same day, Odette had taken each cast member's measurements—even height and weight—which she recorded on a form that included physical traits and a photo. Later, she met one-on-one with each individual to review the potential wardrobe options.

Harriet found the entire process fascinating, especially since Odette also offered hairstyle and makeup suggestions. During the fittings, however, she could turn into a martinet, with her admonitions to stand tall and walk with purpose.

She also had a rare gift for drawing out the other person without revealing too much about herself. Harriet didn't even know where Odette lived when she wasn't on the road, though she'd asked her that question during at least one of the fittings.

"I wonder if you could solve a mystery for me." Odette fixed her gaze on the stage as she spoke. Her profile seemed set in stone. "Even though I'm not a neighbor nor a friend."

An involuntary shiver zipped along Harriet's nerve endings, and she rubbed her arm to still the impulses. "What mystery?"

After a long silence, which Harriet vowed not to break no matter how uncomfortable she became, Odette turned to her with an apologetic smile. "Perhaps some secrets should stay secret. No matter how many plans one makes, one cannot foresee all possible outcomes. Or if what is intended for good will turn out for ill."

"I suppose not," Harriet said, though she had no idea what Odette was talking about. "Though without knowing the circumstances—"

The auditorium lights suddenly brightened, and a voice shouted from the hidden catwalk above the stage. "There are two, make that three, burned-out light bulbs up here."

A second voice, coming from the wings of the stage, responded. "I'll see if there are any extras in the storage room. Stay there till I get back."

"Will do." The person on the catwalk whistled a jaunty tune that Harriet didn't recognize.

However, she recognized the voices. Joshua Corbin and his brother Caleb, born less than a year apart and now in their late teens, had been hired by Joel as the stage crew. Their mother, Ruby, owned a fabric store located close to Poppy Schofield's Biscuit Bistro in the historic section of White Church Bay. Despite the twenty-year gap in their ages, Ruby was one of Aunt Jinny's closest friends.

Since the Corbins didn't have any pets, Harriet scarcely knew the brothers. In fact, she had a difficult time telling them apart even though they weren't twins. But so did Aunt Jinny, who'd known them since they were newborns, and almost everyone else in the community. The brothers were notorious for taking advantage of their uncanny resemblance to each other to avoid trouble.

Or to cause it.

Their Old Testament namesakes were the only two spies who believed the Israelites could drive the Canaanites out of the Promised Land. The other ten disagreed, and because of that, the Israelites spent another forty years wandering in the wilderness. After Moses died, Joshua led the Israelites back to their land of milk and honey. He and Caleb were the only ones of their generation still alive after that long sojourn.

Those who knew the Corbin brothers, famous for their rowdy behavior, often remarked that they were nothing like the Joshua and Caleb from Scripture. But Will once told Harriet he wasn't so sure they didn't share a few strengths with those ancient heroes. "They're independent and imaginative thinkers," he'd said, "with the confidence to stand up for their convictions. Sometimes they need a little guidance, that's all."

Harriet prayed he was right, because those boys sure did enjoy their mischief-making.

"The rehearsal will begin soon," Odette said, drawing Harriet from her thoughts, "and you'll want a few moments to yourself to prepare."

"What about your mystery?" Harriet asked.

"I'll give that more thought." Odette raised her eyes in the direction of the unseen catwalk. "Do you believe things happen for a reason?"

Harriet didn't need the skills of a sleuth to understand Odette's meaning. She obviously regretted bringing up mysteries and secrets. The interruption by the Corbin brothers had given her the out she wanted.

"It often seems that way," Harriet agreed, though she doubted that God had arranged for light bulbs to burn out to put a stop to their conversation. "If you change your mind, give me a call."

"You're most kind. No wonder everyone likes you." Odette spoke in her usual unrushed, languid tone, with her sentences flowing into one another so that Harriet didn't have an opportunity to respond without appearing rude. "And my wish to see you before I left for the day has been answered. We must make an appointment for tomorrow afternoon. The gown Elizabeth wears for the dance with Mr. Darcy is ready to be fitted."

Was the appointment an excuse to give them the opportunity to talk in private? Or had Odette decided against seeking Harriet's help? She'd have to wait until tomorrow to find out.

"The clinic closes at noon," Harriet said. "Two o'clock or any time after that would be fine."

"I'll see you at two then." Odette left the auditorium through the same door she'd entered. With the lights turned up, however, the deep shadows that had concealed her arrival no longer existed.

"Found them," a Corbin brother shouted.

The one on the catwalk stopped whistling. "'Bout time. Bring 'em on up so we can get 'em changed before they start rehearsin'."

Harriet sank into a nearby seat. Odette was right—she should be using this time to prepare for the opening scene of the play. It was difficult to concentrate on her character, however, after the strange conversation she'd had with the mysterious costume designer.

"There you are." Will sauntered toward her. "The buffet is open. You want to eat now, or wait for a break?"

Harriet met him halfway up the aisle and wrapped her arm around his. "Now. Once rehearsals start, Elizabeth will be too nervous to eat."

Will chuckled then paused by one of the back rows. "Before we join the others, let me tell you about my conversation with Joel."

"You told him about Dankworth?"

"He doesn't want to pursue it. He won't tell Van, and he asked us not to say anything either."

Harriet could hardly believe what she was hearing. "Why not?"

"He has no proof, so it'd be his word against Dankworth's should he deny it. Which he probably would." Will took Harriet's hands in his. "Plus, Joel doesn't want to risk making an enemy."

"I think he already has one."

"Maybe. But an accusation without any proof won't resolve anything."

Harriet admitted Will was right as they headed for the lobby. They got in line for the deli buffet behind Garth and Elena and were soon in conversation about the three hedgehog babies—or hoglets—who were the newest residents at the wildlife center. A short time later, Joel herded the Act One cast into the auditorium. The rehearsal went well, and Harriet didn't hear any talk of the opening of the play being delayed or of sounds that went bump in the night.

Her only regret was that she didn't get a chance to talk to Kezia, who seemed to be back to her practical, sensible self, or to do any behind-the-scenes exploring. She was fairly certain Van hadn't gotten a chance to do that either.

They arrived home to a warm welcome from Maxwell, who yipped with joy at seeing them. Charlie and Ash greeted them too, but with more dignity. Once all the last-of-the-night chores were done, Harriet joined Will on the sofa with her folder of documents.

"I've been waiting all afternoon and evening to read Eugenie's letter." She'd already told him as they drove to the theater what she'd learned from Mrs. Atkins and Colleen and the *Whitby Gazette* articles.

She snuggled close to Will, slid the copy of the letter from the folder, and began to read aloud.

> *My dearest Layla,*
>
> *All the time I played—and quite successfully if I do say so myself—the oh-so-perfect Elizabeth who could do no wrong in her father's eyes, I longed to follow in Lydia's footsteps and her carriage ride all the way to Gretna Green.*
>
> *So when he proposed, how could I say no?*
>
> *Surely you know who I mean. As Lydia says, "If you cannot guess with who, I shall think you a simpleton, for there is but one man in the world I love, and he is an angel." But I know you can guess. You're smart enough to have seen what everyone else hasn't.*

You and I have bright futures ahead of us, each in our own way, don't we? I'll write again once our plans are set. For now, all we care about is being with each other and shutting ourselves away from the outside world for as long as possible.

With love,
Eugenie

After Harriet finished reading the letter, she handed it to Will. "What do you think?" she asked.

"Despite not mentioning the name of the man she ran away with, it's fairly straightforward. Who is this Layla?"

Harriet pulled the police interview from her folder and skimmed the info. "According to this, her name is Layla Hastings. Nineteen years old. Home address in Plymouth. This says she was an apprentice seamstress, but the newspaper article said the letter was sent to another actress."

"I suppose even our beloved *Gazette* makes the odd mistake now and again," Will said.

Harriet acknowledged his comment with a smile then finished reading the report. "She'd been with the troupe for less than a year."

"Did Layla say who Eugenie ran off with?"

"She insisted she didn't know. Apparently, the police finally gave up asking."

Will reached for a wrapped toffee from a nearby candy dish. "Perhaps they were so relieved to have proof that Eugenie hadn't been kidnapped, or something even worse, that they closed the case without verifying what the letter said. Look at the situation from their point of view. Now they could assure the community that there were no monsters lurking about the moors."

"I suppose they expected Eugenie to return to the troupe. Or at least to show up somewhere."

"Eugenie must have expected that too." Will ran his finger down the page till he reached the sentence he wanted. "'You and I have bright futures ahead of us.' Sounds to me like she planned to return to the theater. Maybe not immediately, but sometime."

"Colleen told me she did an extensive internet search for Eugenie." Harriet snatched her cell phone from the nightstand. "But she didn't have the police report, so she didn't know Layla's name. She couldn't have tried to find her."

Will placed his hand over Harriet's before she could open her internet app.

"It's getting late. How about we wait until tomorrow for any more sleuthing."

Harriet reluctantly agreed. But as she got ready for bed, her thoughts returned to Odette and the interruption to their conversation caused by the Corbin brothers. Though Harriet appreciated Will's optimistic point of view about them, Joshua and Caleb had a well-deserved reputation as mischievous troublemakers.

Harriet had once suspected them of playing silly tricks on the shop owners near their mother's fabric store. Even Ruby wondered if they were the ones mixing up the yarns with the quilt squares and the cross-stitch kits with the macramé in what was a true locked-room mystery.

They'd been innocent then, but what if they were up to their mischievous tricks now? Could they be responsible for the strange noises and the blasts of cold air?

Had the prank-playing brothers created Kezia's ghost?

Journal Entry
October 28, 1985

The letter arrived today, which means I can finally breathe again. The not knowing has been horrible, but we agreed there'd be no phone calls. We can't take that chance. Not when the stakes are so high and our foe is so sneaky.

I saw him outside the post office, watching and waiting. He frightens me even though I know he doesn't know our plans. And, in the long run, it doesn't matter if he reads the letter. I'll be taking it to the police later, and the search for Eugenie will end.

It only matters that he doesn't see the envelope. Because then he'll know the letter didn't come from Gretna Green.

CHAPTER EIGHT

Saturday's clinic schedule left no time for idle moments, especially since Polly wasn't there to check in and check out patients. Though she usually worked on Saturdays, she'd scheduled a rare day off before the appointment calendar filled up. Harriet didn't have the heart to ask her to change the plans she'd already made with Van and her parents. Throughout the morning hours, Harriet moved patients in and out of the exam rooms, listened to heartbeats, took temps, and administered vaccinations.

Eleven-year-old Winifred Wilkerson and seven-year-old Jack Lancaster stopped by to ask Harriet for help with Jack's school project on why it was best to leave wild animals that appeared to be lost alone unless they were injured. Their shared love of exploring the moors and knack for finding injured animals had made them the best of friends despite their age difference. Harriet had taught them that not all "lost animals" are truly lost and that most could find their way home if left alone. The two children were accompanied by Gideon, Jack's golden retriever and constant companion.

In between saying goodbye to the children and tending to the next patient, Harriet checked the phone system for any messages. She deleted the call from a robotic spammer, saved the message from their medical supplies vendor for Polly to return on Monday, and then listened to the third and final message.

"Hi, Harriet." A soft voice with its distinct Yorkshire accent sounded through the speaker. "This is Martha Banks. I'm sorry to bother you on a Saturday, but I have somewhat of a situation here. Do you think you could come by sometime this afternoon? I'll be home all day."

A situation?

What in the world could Martha mean by that?

Besides caring for the animals on her hobby farm, the petite, silver-haired woman also provided a home for injured wildlife. Shortly after Harriet arrived in Yorkshire, Martha had taken in a baby deer after Will accidentally hit its mother with his previous vehicle, an old funeral hearse. Only a few months ago, she'd provided a temporary home for the injured pine marten that Winifred, Jack, and Fern Chapman had found.

Harriet immediately dialed Martha's number and ended up leaving a message of her own. "Be there soon," she promised, wishing Martha hadn't been so cryptic.

Did the situation involve one of her goats or sheep? Or an animal, domestic or wild, under her special care?

Either way, Harriet found it odd Martha hadn't been more specific.

"Maybe she wants to talk about something altogether different," Harriet said to Maxwell, who was sprawled on his bed beneath the desk. "At least she didn't say it was an emergency. I just pray it's not a 'volunteer opportunity.'"

Or anything else that would require Harriet to say no to the friend who'd protected the pine marten during his recovery and was among the small circle who knew where on the moors an entire colony of the nearly extinct species could be found.

Within a half hour of closing the clinic, Harriet had placed her veterinary bag in the Beast. She'd also packed a change of clothes so she could drive straight from Martha's farm to the Beacon for her appointment with Odette Jones.

Over her first cup of coffee that morning, Harriet conducted an internet search for Layla Hastings and came up empty. Colleen, with more resources at her fingertips, might have better luck. Depending on how long the fitting with Odette took, Harriet had a vague plan to see if Colleen could meet at the newspaper office for a joint research session later that day.

Given that the *Whitby Gazette* was closed on Saturdays and Harriet didn't have Colleen's phone number, the likelihood of that happening wasn't very good. Her second, and more likely-to-succeed plan, was to persuade Van to run Layla's name through his database.

All Harriet needed was an address or a phone number. Then she could figure out a way to talk to Layla in person.

Why did she feel the need to talk to the woman?

That question wouldn't go away. And Harriet didn't have an answer for it. The handwritten note from Eugenie obviously convinced the police that she was safe and sound in Scotland. Harriet didn't fault them for coming to that conclusion. As Will had said, they probably were relieved to know their community hadn't been infiltrated by an unnamed evil. Life could return to the norm of unlocked doors and children roaming the moors.

But from her perspective, there were just too many holes in Eugenie's case, too many unanswered questions. Two, especially, stood above all the others.

Question One: Who was the man Eugenie ran away with?

Eugenie's note, which echoed the words written by Lydia to her friend, Mrs. Forster, indicated that Layla knew the identity of the groom. Yet Layla insisted to the police that she did not.

Was she lying? Or had Eugenie overestimated her friend's deductive abilities? Neither the police nor the press seemed to have made any extra efforts to find out.

Question Two: Who were the men Eugenie talked to at the Crow's Nest? Nothing in the police reports or the newspaper articles that Harriet read mentioned the encounter at all.

The need to know the answers to those questions created an itch Harriet couldn't scratch.

So why did she need to find Layla Hastings?

Because that was the only way she'd find out who accompanied Eugenie to Gretna Green.

Harriet turned onto Martha's lane and parked beside the picturesque two-story farmhouse. Low box hedges lined the edge of the well-tended lawn. In the spring and summer, the huge limbs of an ancient chestnut tree sheltered the bench encircling the trunk. Now, though, the sea breezes set the red, orange, and golden leaves to dancing until they loosened their hold on the branches and drifted to the ground.

As Harriet slid from the driver's seat, Martha strolled toward her. Her thick gorgeous hair hung in a long silver braid over her shoulder. She wore a brown flannel shirt with a purple tee, and heavy jeans tucked into Wellies. She welcomed Harriet with a dazzling smile and warm greeting.

"Thanks for coming out. I hope I didn't ruin any afternoon plans."

"Not at all," Harriet replied. "Will is busy with preparations for the autumn bazaar. Poppy has a huge list of things for him to do. I'm meeting the costume designer at the theater later this afternoon, but that's it."

"You're in *Pride and Prejudice*? How fun that must be. Who do you play?"

"Elizabeth Bennet, if you can believe it. I'm sure I'm more suited to play the lady's maid. But the director is an old friend of Will's, and he's promised to make me twenty again."

"Is that so?" Martha's gentle laugh was a sweet balm. "Do you think he could do that for me?" She sucked in her cheeks then laughed again. "Those days are long behind me and, to be honest, I don't need to see them again."

"Neither do I," Harriet admitted, thinking back to her college years. Though she had fond memories of football games, pizza parties, and internships, she'd also carried heavy loads that required hours and hours in the library. "I feel like I'm living my best days right now."

"That's because you are. I felt that way when I was your age, and I still feel that way today. If you ask me, that's the secret to happy living." Martha's pleasant smile faded. "Though you didn't come out here to talk philosophy."

"Your message said something about a situation," Harriet prompted.

"It's true." Martha gestured toward the long barn located farther up the lane. "Shall we?"

If anyone ever thought to ask Harriet to choose her favorite Yorkshire barn, this one, with its red-tiled roof and crimson door, would definitely be her number-one choice. The multitude of windows, with their wooden frames painted a bright cheery blue, allowed fresh air and sunshine into the barn in the summer when they were wide open and kept out the autumn chill now that they were closed.

As Martha stooped to pick up a fallen branch from the lane, she asked, "What do you know about the Scottish Kellas?"

Harriet's jaw dropped. "You have a Kellas cat?"

"I think so," Martha replied as they continued walking toward the barn. "I've never seen one before, but I looked up photographs online. Though I could be wrong and she's simply an oversized black cat."

"Where did you get her?"

"Someone left her in a crate at the end of my lane." Martha shrugged. "It happens more than you think, though usually I find a dog or cat inside. Sometimes a rabbit or an injured bird. People who can't be troubled to do the right thing know they can count on me to do it for them."

She paused a moment then said, "Though I suppose, in a way, they're doing the right thing by abandoning their unwanted animals here instead of by the side of a country road or out on the moors."

"You have a big heart, Martha. And a multitude of stars in your crown."

While carrying on the conversation, Harriet also searched her memory for every tidbit of information she'd ever read or heard about Kellas cats. "Is she injured?"

"From what I could see, no. But she's a wild one. Too wild for me do any kind of hands-on examination."

"That's not unusual, is it? Aren't they primarily feral?"

"Practically untamable, from what I've read," Martha said. "The Scottish wildcat often dominates the domesticity of the ordinary house cat."

"I'm amazed a Scottish wildcat would be anywhere around here. Aren't they on the Critically Endangered List?"

Martha chuckled. "I never expected to see a pine marten around here either. They're even rarer than Scottish wildcats, and yet one was a temporary guest of mine only a few short months ago."

They'd reached the barn, and Martha pushed open the huge sliding door. "Besides, we don't have any idea where this cat came from or where she was found. Her parents could be a hundred kilometers or more away from here."

Harriet readily agreed. She was eager to see the Kellas cat and also to research the unusual offspring that came from a Scottish wildcat mating with an ordinary house cat. The hybrids were causing almost as much harm, if not more, to the purity of the wildcat species as was disease, loss of habitat, and accidental deaths such as being killed by automobiles.

Though she couldn't remember the exact statistic, Harriet seemed to recall that experts believed that most, if not all, Scottish wildcats had a house cat somewhere in their genealogy. The Kellas cat was a specific type of what scientists termed an interspecific hybrid and not a cat breed such as a Persian, Siamese, or—Harriet's personal favorite—a Maine Coon.

As she entered the well-lit barn, Harriet marveled as she always did at the lack of cobwebs in the rafters and dirt in the corners.

How Martha managed such a feat was unimaginable, but somehow she did.

"She's in the isolation area." Martha led the way to a tiny corner room with a set of cabinets below a metal counter lining one wall. Three enclosures with wire fronts and of varying lengths, built to accommodate different-sized animals, sat on top of the counter. An empty, heavy-duty plastic crate, no doubt the one left at the end of the lane, rested on the floor.

The ebony cat huddled on a blanket in the far corner of the enclosure. Though she didn't make a sound, her green eyes glared at her captors.

"How did you move her?" Harriet asked. She was an expert at handling animals that didn't want to be handled, but even she would be leery of opening a crate with the obviously angry Kellas cat inside.

"The oldest trick in the book," Martha replied. "Bribery. I put food and water in the enclosure then put the open doors together. She was still hesitant to leave the devil she knew for the devil she didn't, so I tilted the crate and prayed she'd slide into the enclosure and not to the floor."

The bottom of the small bowl still contained a smattering of canned cat food. "How much would you say she ate?"

"One entire tin and half of another. The single-serving size, mind you, not ones the size of a soup tin."

"She was starving," Harriet murmured to herself as she scrutinized the cat. Her coat was entirely black except for a small scruff of white at her neck that resembled a cloud puff. Though she appeared young, she was definitely bigger than a typical cat, even from one of the larger breeds. Another distinctive feature was her narrow and elongated head shape."

"What's your expert opinion?" Martha asked. "Is she a Kellas?"

"I'm not a hundred percent sure."

"How about eighty?" Martha teased.

"I'll go as high as eighty-five. Probably even ninety. I believe I read something about Kellas cats in one of Grandad's journals after I moved here. He was fascinated by the folklore."

"You mean like the cat-sìth?" Martha asked.

"I'm not familiar with that term." Harriet frowned as she tried to recall what she'd read. "Grandad wrote about a Scottish myth that says a ghost cat haunts the Highlands. Its description matches that of a Kellas."

"I hadn't heard of a cat-sìth either until this morning. The name is rooted in Celtic mythology and means 'fairy cat.'"

"A fairy cat doesn't sound very dangerous. But a cat-sìth? I'm not sure I want to encounter something called that." Harriet let out a deep sigh as she considered how best to examine the Kellas. "As much as I hate to sedate her, it's the only way I can I examine her."

"That seems the safest, wisest course to me," Martha agreed.

Harriet glanced at her watch. "I told Odette I'd be at the theater by two. If it's okay with you, I'll go to the fitting, pick up a few things I need from the clinic, then come back."

"That sounds fine. Neither of us is going anywhere," Martha assured Harriet. She pointed at a camera. "I can monitor her from my kitchen. She was asleep until we woke her up. I imagine she'll sleep again once we're gone."

"That may be the best medicine. Along with the food."

As the women returned to Harriet's vehicle, Martha said, "My late husband and I went to the Beacon for a matinee performance of *Pride and Prejudice*. I haven't given much thought to those days in ages. But I remember how shocked we all were when that young actress went missing. I wonder whatever happened to her."

"Apparently she eloped." Harriet placed her veterinary bag in the back seat of the Beast.

Martha's eyebrows rose in surprise. "I don't remember hearing that, though I suppose I must have. Too caught up in my own wedding plans, I suppose, though that seems terribly self-centered of me, doesn't it?"

"But totally understandable." From her own recent firsthand experience, Harriet could relate to the single-minded focus a wedding caused. "She wrote a note to a friend, a seamstress working for the troupe, and gave her the news."

"I'm glad to hear it. She was such a nice young woman. We ran into her at the White Hart that Friday evening of the big storm. We were engaged then and celebrating the two-year anniversary of the day we met. She was gracious enough to sign the menu card for me. It was such a kindness, especially since she was in quite the hurry."

As if on cue, Harriet's inner tingles sparked to life. "You must have been one of the last to see her before she left," she exclaimed. "Did you tell the police?"

Martha tilted her head as if to better see into the past. "It was such a long time ago. But I believe someone interviewed my husband. Not that we knew anything that could have been of help. She didn't tell us she was leaving, and we had no reason to suspect anything."

"Was she with anyone? A man?" Before Martha could answer, Harriet explained about Eugenie's letter to Layla Hastings and her interview with the police. "As far as I know, no one knew who he was."

"I'll have to think back on that day while you're gone," Martha continued. "See if I can't recall more of the details. I'll search for that menu card too, if you're interested in seeing it."

"Please do," Harriet enthused. "That is, if it's not too much bother."

"I have an idea or two where to look. Who knows? It might help me remember more about that day than how excited I was to talk to a real-life actress."

They chatted for a few more minutes, then Harriet drove toward the Beacon-on-the-Moor Playhouse. She hoped the fitting wouldn't take too long. Not only was she eager to talk more with Martha, but she was also concerned about the Scottish Kellas.

But the nearer Harriet got to the theater, the more her thoughts drifted away from the cat and toward Eugenie and Layla, Kezia's ghost, the Corbin brothers, and the haunting noise she'd heard when she thought she was alone in the auditorium.

She'd started to tell Will about the strange sound a couple of times, but for some inexplicable reason, she couldn't form the words. He'd believe her—of that she had no doubt. Still, she found the whole thing embarrassing. And how could she ever explain Odette's spectral appearance? That'd been more unnerving than the noise.

"And she knew it," Harriet said aloud. As if she'd hid in the shadows on purpose. Yet she hadn't admitted to hearing anything.

Was Odette somehow "haunting" the theater?

Executive Log Entry
October 31, 1985

SH still in hospital. Weakling. At least he knows not to cross me again. Bonus news: now that the Beacon is ruined, that simpering actress ran off with some other poor sop. I was right about her. Nothing more than another money-grubbing social climber trying to best her betters. She was smart to listen to the messengers I sent. Good riddance.

CHAPTER NINE

Harriet hurried to the backstage room set aside for the costumes. In the theater's original design, according to old blueprints that Joel had found in the county archives, this space was the rehearsal room and the costume storage area was upstairs. But Joel's limited budget meant that the theater's upper level was in Phase Two of his renovation plans.

For now, the needed upgrades to the main level were his priority. Whether Phase Two ever moved from design plans to reality was dependent on the Beacon's success in the community.

The current costume room bustled with energy as Harriet stepped across the threshold. Wheeled racks of dresses and cloaks and gowns stood hither and thither without any sense of order that she could see. Dressing screens were angled in each corner of the room, and mirrors covered an entire wall.

"Dear Harriet. You've arrived." Odette greeted her with a tape measure in one hand and a pin cushion on her wrist.

To Harriet's surprise, Odette stood next to Polly, who giggled and finger-waved as she swayed back and forth in a gold-colored gown. Wasn't she supposed to be spending the day with her family?

"The play takes priority," Polly said, as if she'd read Harriet's mind. "Even Mum and Dad said so."

Elena and Kezia were also in the room, along with Ruby Corbin, who'd apparently been enlisted to assist with the fittings and sewing.

"I'm sorry I'm a few minutes late," Harriet said. "I was on a vet call."

"Anything serious?" Polly asked.

"Nope."

Polly's eyes briefly widened. Perhaps she'd answered a tad too quickly, Harriet reflected, though she doubted anyone else had noticed. Martha didn't say to keep the Kellas cat a secret, but Harriet's natural discretion when it came to her clients kept her from telling the roomful of women about the mysterious feline. Scottish Kellas cats might not be as scarce as pine martens, but they were still a novelty, and she didn't want curiosity-seekers showing up at Martha's farm.

"As far as I'm concerned, you're right on time. What matters most is you're joining our little party." Odette tugged the fabric at Polly's waist then glided to a nearby rack. She removed two hangers and held up both gowns for Harriet's perusal. "Both of these are suitable for your coloring and the ball where Elizabeth dances with Mr. Darcy for the first time. Do you have a preference?"

Harriet studied the two lovely dresses and chose the sapphire-blue one.

"Isn't that Will's favorite color?" Polly teased.

"I see you're wearing yellow. Isn't that Van's favorite?" Harriet retorted. Both women laughed.

Even Odette smiled. Today she wore a gray and blue scarf fashionably draped over a navy-blue pullover with charcoal-gray slacks. Dark blues, grays, and blacks were definitely the designer's go-to wardrobe choices. Harriet couldn't recall ever seeing her dressed in any other colors. Perhaps creams or ivories as accent colors, but no pastels or jewel tones. Those palettes were for the actresses.

"Get thee behind a screen and try it on," Odette faux-ordered. While neither her shrewd gaze nor her perfect posture faltered, her demeanor seemed more relaxed than it had been the evening before.

Harriet doubted she'd learn anything about Odette's mystery today, not with so many other people around. Hopefully, that also meant Odette wouldn't bring up Harriet's moment of fright in the auditorium either. That would be too embarrassing.

As conversations buzzed on the other side of the screen, Harriet changed into the blue gown. As the swaths of fabric slid over her head and skimmed her body, she could almost feel herself being transported to the early years of the nineteenth century. Except for the length, the dress seemed tailor-made for her. Even before she looked in the mirror, she felt absolutely beautiful.

She held up the skirt so she wouldn't trip and stepped from behind the screen. The gasps from the other women assured her that she'd made the perfect choice.

"Ooh-la-la," Odette exclaimed in a perfect French-Creole accent. "You were made for this dress."

"It's gorgeous," Harriet replied.

"It gives you confidence, no? You will play this scene with perfection because, dressed in this way, you are no longer Harriet Bailey-Knight, the esteemed veterinarian, but Miss Elizabeth Bennet, a gentleman's daughter who is most worthy to be dancing with the proud and prejudiced Mr. Darcy."

Odette spoke with such passion that Harriet and the others applauded her. She accepted their tribute with a regal nod of her head then pointed to the shoe rack.

"Find your shoes, Lizzy." Odette traded the French accent for her usual sophisticated tone. "Then stand on the hemming stool so I can set the pins. We can't have you tripping in front of your dance partner."

The shoes and boots were already arranged on the racks by actor. Harriet had three pairs—one for "everyday," one for walking in the mud when she visited the very sick Jane at Netherfield, and her party shoes. All the women's shoes had either flat or low heels. "It might surprise you to know," Odette had said to them, "that high heels for women were not in fashion in the early nineteenth century."

Harriet slipped on the black flats then stepped onto the low stool. Odette immediately got to work adjusting and pinning the fabric while Harriet did her best to stand still with her arms at her side.

Over Odette's head, she caught Kezia glancing at her. Harriet smiled in return, and Kezia lowered her gaze and bit her bottom lip. Harriet longed to have a moment to talk with her in private but didn't see how that would be possible.

Especially since Kezia was now disappearing behind a screen to change out of her "Charlotte Lucas is married to Mr. Collins and living at the Hunsford parsonage near Rosings Park" costume. She'd probably be leaving soon, while Harriet was trapped on the hemming stool.

Sure enough, just moments later, Kezia emerged from behind the screen dressed in a hip-length oversized sweater over skinny jeans tucked into ankle boots. On her way out, she paused beside the stool.

"Andrew is helping Joel make a decision on a few of the props," she said to Harriet, "so I'll be sticking around for a few minutes. When you're finished, would you mind joining us?"

The pointed look in Kezia's eyes made it clear that the props were an excuse. Apparently, she was as eager for a private talk with Harriet as Harriet was for a private talk with her.

"Sounds fun," she replied.

"Stand still," Odette hissed.

"Sorry. I didn't realize I'd moved." Harriet made an "eek" face, taking care Odette didn't see it, and Kezia responded with a conspiratorial grin. The breakthrough moment warmed Harriet's heart. Though she and Kezia had never been close friends, their casual relationship had chilled when Harriet had suspected Andrew of impersonating the ghost knight.

Andrew, whose main concern was catching the real culprit, had been gracious and forgiving. Kezia, who'd been away visiting her mother at the time, not so much.

Harriet guessed the only reason Kezia had told her about seeing her ghost was because Harriet had been standing near the wings. Otherwise, Kezia never would have chosen to confide in her.

"I'd love to see the props," Harriet said, careful to stand still as a statue. "Andrew is the perfect person to oversee that task."

Though his shop could by no means be described as upscale, all kinds of wondrous and unusual objects could be found there. Even a few of more value than one would guess by looking at them. Besides the historical items he could glean from his shop, he also knew all the longtime families in the area. Many of them had antique lanterns, candlesticks, bed-warmers, and coal scuttles. Harriet herself had objects from that time period scattered throughout her home.

"Great," Kezia said, easing her grin into a warm smile. "We're using the workroom at the other end of the corridor to sort through everything."

After Kezia left, Polly perched on a tall stool while she waited for Ruby to finish the alterations on one of Jane Bennet's morning gowns, a lovely lavender floral that scooped too low at the neckline for Polly's comfort.

"I think it's so romantic," she said to no one in particular, "how Joel chose married couples to play couples. Van and me as Mr. Bingley and Jane. Harriet and Will as Elizabeth and Mr. Darcy. Kezia and Andrew as Charlotte and Mr. Collins."

"Don't forget Elena and Garth as Lydia and Mr. Wickham," Ruby said. "They may not be married yet, but I'll be surprised if they're not engaged before the end of the year. It makes me so happy to see the two of them and little Jack sitting together in church every Sunday as if they're already a family."

"I'm not sure romance had anything to do with Joel's decision," Harriet said. "He had a more practical motive."

"How so?" Polly asked.

"He's working with amateurs," Harriet explained, "and casting couples to play opposite each other gives our performances an automatic boost. We already have a connection with each other. He also said something to Will about how helpful it is for us to rehearse our scenes with each other on our own time. It's easier for us to memorize our lines."

"That makes sense." Polly played with her wedding band. "Van and I have had a lot of fun acting out our scenes. Especially the proposal."

Harriet smiled. The path to love and marriage had not been a smooth one for her young friend and the heartsick constable. That made what Polly said about rehearsing Bingley's proposal all the more poignant, since she'd broken up with Van the first time he asked her to marry him.

And had been absolutely miserable afterward.

When he'd suffered injuries carrying an arsonist out of a burning cottage, she rarely left his side during his hospitalization, even though she was recovering at the time from being hit by a car while riding her bike.

"Please stop with the fidgets." Odette peered up at Harriet. "I've known four-year-olds who could stand still longer than you."

Harriet muttered another apology then focused on a blotchy spot on the far wall. She felt Polly's gaze on her but feared sneaking a glance at her friend. If she did, they might wind up as laughing puddles on the floor, and what would the imperious Odette say about that?

After a few beats of silence, Polly spoke again. "I also think it's great that Joel's first production is *Pride and Prejudice* when he could have chosen some off-off-Broadway play. P&P is the perfect classic to launch the Beacon."

"He wants to pay homage to the past." Harriet made sure she stayed statue-still while she spoke. "Almost like 'the show must go on' even if forty years goes by in the meantime."

At that moment Odette's shoulders stiffened, and she dropped a pin. She snapped it up and jabbed it into the fabric.

Harriet froze, and her mind whirled. Had she or Polly said something to upset Odette?

Surely not. She must have gotten lost in her own thoughts as she was performing the routine task. Perhaps the mystery she'd alluded to last night was weighing on her mind.

"All done," Ruby said as she shook out Jane's dress then held it up to Polly's shoulders. "This should do the trick."

As Polly changed from the golden-yellow frock into the lavender morning gown, Odette finished pinning Harriet's hem. She stood back while Harriet maneuvered a careful spin on the stool, then directed her to the corridor. With Odette standing outside the wardrobe room door and scrutinizing her every move, Harriet walked past the dressing rooms, turned when directed, and returned.

"Perfection," Odette declared, complimenting her own work with absolutely no sense of conceit. She smiled. "You do Elizabeth proud. Do not doubt Mr. Elphick's casting choice."

Touched by the unexpected kindness, Harriet smiled back at her. "Is my insecurity that obvious?"

"Only to those of us who've spent most of their lives treading the boards." Odette checked the time on her wristwatch. "I must be off, but I'll return later to hem the dress. If you'd be so kind as to place it on a hanger once you've changed?"

Harriet readily agreed then followed Odette back into the wardrobe room where Ruby was fussing with Polly's morning dress. Odette retrieved her bag from a cupboard while Harriet went behind the screen to change. As she removed the dress shoes, she heard the murmur of voices, but by the time she emerged from the screen, Odette was gone and Polly was behind her own screen.

Ruby offered to take care of the gown, and Harriet gladly handed it over to her. A moment later, Polly joined them, and Ruby took her dress too. Both women thanked her, said their goodbyes, and entered the corridor.

Polly shuffle-danced to the first dressing room door. "Did you see this?" she exclaimed. She gestured to the door's sign like a television model showcasing a prize.

A wave of excitement swept through Harriet. Their names plus two more were listed in large block letters along with their roles:

Elena Hazeldine
Lydia Bennet

Harriet Bailey-Knight
Elizabeth Bennet

Ada Winslow
Mrs. Bennet

Polly Worthington
Jane Bennet

"What fun," Harriet exclaimed. "I'm so glad they put us together."

"Me too. Especially considering this." Polly pointed to the other two dressing rooms. The sign on the middle door read, WOMEN'S CAST. The sign on the last door read, MEN'S CAST.

"Everyone else has to share?" Harriet was both flabbergasted and honored. "Why do we get our own room?"

As soon as she asked the question, she realized the answer.

"Because we're the stars." Polly grabbed Harriet's hands and practically jumped up and down. "I've always wanted to be a star. All this is becoming so much more real. I can't wait until we're in front of an audience."

Harriet laughed at Polly's enthusiasm. Seeing her name on the door only moments after wearing a gown that practically screamed "You are Elizabeth" added a dose of reality to the dream of being on stage and, unlike Polly's reaction, scared Harriet half to death.

"Even better, our dressing room is the best one." Polly opened the door with their names on it and pulled Harriet into the room. She gestured to another door opening into a bathroom. "See? This is the only one with a private loo. We don't have to use the ones in the hall. We even have a shower."

Polly's infectious giggle caused Harriet to ignore her nerves and grin with the delight of it all. She turned away from the bathroom to gaze at the rest of the space. A small sofa and two chairs surrounded a round coffee table on the far wall while four vintage dressing tables and lighted mirrors were situated around the room. Calligraphy script adorned ivory cards tucked into the frames of the mirrors.

"We've already been assigned vanities," Harriet said, pointing to the card bearing her name. "This one's mine." She gingerly lowered herself to the chair as if she were afraid it would disappear. Strange, how magical a place the theater's backstage seemed to be. Once she was safely seated, she stared at her reflection then turned on the lights surrounding the mirror. Every one of her laugh lines suddenly deepened.

Despite Odette's encouraging words, Harriet once again questioned how she could play a character who was so young. She glanced at Polly, who was sitting at her own table and making dramatic facial expressions in front of her mirror.

If only Harriet was Jane and Polly was Elizabeth. Too late for that to happen now. And even if they could switch, that would mean Will and Van would have to switch too.

Okay, technically they wouldn't *have* to switch, but Harriet didn't want to pretend to love Van any more than Polly would want to pretend to love Will.

Besides, Will made such a perfect Mr. Darcy, and not because she was biased or because his first name was actually Fitzwilliam.

With his sweet and pleasant temperament, Van lacked the aristocratic bearing needed for the role. No matter how hard he tried, he could never be a believable Mr. Darcy.

Harriet turned off the lights and opened the vanity drawers. The top center drawer held a brand-new makeup kit, a variety of brushes, makeup remover, and facial cloths. The two drawers on each side of the knee space were empty.

"Mrs. Atkins's granddaughter refinished these tables," Harriet said to Polly. "Didn't she do a beautiful job?"

"Kezia is so talented at this kind of thing," Polly replied. "I wish I could take one of these home with me."

Harriet about fell out of the chair. "Kezia is the Atkinses' granddaughter? How could I not have known that?"

"Because the Ellsworths don't have pets for you to ooh and aah over," Polly teased.

Before Harriet could reply, a boom reverberated throughout the building. Both she and Polly dropped to the floor and stared at the open door.

"What was that?" Polly whispered. She pulled her phone from her pocket. "I'm calling Van."

Harriet's mind raced through options and possibilities. Should they leave this room or stay put? Most likely Ruby was still in the wardrobe room and the Ellsworths and Joel were at the opposite end of the corridor in the storage room. Had Odette made it out of the building already?

What if someone needed medical attention? Aunt Jinny was across the Channel—no way could she help in this emergency.

Oh, God, Harriet silently prayed. *Help me know what to do.*

CHAPTER TEN

Harriet peeked into the hallway, Polly huddled next to her, and saw Ruby looking out from the wardrobe room. The next moment Ruby scurried to the dressing room and gripped Harriet's hand.

"What's going on?" she whispered, her voice trembling with fear. She looked past Harriet toward the opposite end of the corridor. "There's Joel."

The three women stayed huddled together in the doorway as Joel, followed by Andrew and Kezia, hugged the wall and sidled toward them. As he approached, Joel shooed them into the dressing room and closed the door.

"Is everyone okay?" he asked. "Is anyone else in the theater?"

"My boys might be," Ruby said. "They said something about testing the sound system. I'll try to reach them." She stepped away from the group and made the call.

"What about Odette?" Joel asked.

"She left a few minutes ago." Harriet looked at Polly for confirmation.

"At least ten or more." Polly held up her phone. "Van's on speaker. He's on his way."

Joel stepped closer to Polly. "Van, this is Joel. How soon before you get here?"

"Less than five minutes. Are you the only ones in the building?"

Joel shot a glance at Ruby, whose relieved expression said more than a thousand words. "As far as I know, yes."

"There's no need for you or Caleb to come," Ruby said into her phone. "I'm all right, and Constable Worthington will be here soon."

"Did you hear gunfire?" Van asked.

"It sounded more like an explosion to me," Joel said. "I was in the workshop with Andrew and Kezia, and the lights flickered."

"Do you smell or see any smoke?"

"Nothing like that. Listen, Van, I'm going to get everyone outside then take a look around. If there's a fire somewhere, I want to snuff it out before the place burns down."

"I recommend you stay outside with the others," Van said, his tone firm. "Get everyone to a place of safety and stay there. The fire department is right behind me."

Joel frowned then looked around at the others. "You heard the man. The closest exit is the one in the wardrobe room. We'll go out that way."

"Quick as possible," Andrew added. "In case someone's in the building who doesn't belong here."

Joel frowned then cracked open the door. "The hallway's clear," he whispered. "Hurry now."

Harriet and the other women followed after him while Andrew brought up the rear. In less than a minute, though it seemed to Harriet that time turned to a sludge, they'd wended their way between the clothing racks and dressing screens and pushed the bar on the thick exterior door.

It opened onto a walkway that ran along the side of the building with another set of exterior doors at the other end. The group descended the short set of stairs at their end and followed the sidewalk to the driveway. Sirens, growing louder with each passing second, signaled help was on the way.

Joel led the group across the drive to a row of poplars that served as an imperfect barrier to the wind that blew in from the North Sea. Though she had grabbed her jacket as they hurried past the costumes, Harriet still shivered. She and the other women stood close together in front of one of the slender poplars. Joel paced in a tight back-and-forth, as if to expend his excess energy.

"This can't be happening," he muttered as he shook his head in disbelief. "*Why* is this happening?"

Harriet wished she could provide him with an answer. Hopefully, the incident was nothing more than an antiquated system reaching its breaking point. She knew from personal experience that such a repair could be a devastating expense. When she'd first moved into Grandad's house, it seemed that everything that could go wrong did go wrong.

That explanation was definitely preferable to the nefarious one rattling around in her head. The conversation she'd overheard in the diner the day before tied a knot in her stomach.

"I see you," Polly shouted into the phone. She raised her arm high in the air to wave at the vehicles turning into the driveway. "There's Van," she squealed. "And the fire department. Our heroes."

"I see you too." The relief in Van's voice was almost palpable over the speaker. "Stay where you are."

Now that help had arrived, Harriet stepped away from the group to call Will. Since Ruby had already talked with at least one of her sons and the cavalry had been summoned, the White Church Bay grapevine must already be buzzing. She didn't want Will to worry about her for even a second.

Their conversation was brief, since Will, who'd heard the sirens as the emergency vehicles left the village, grabbed his car key the second Harriet told him what happened. By the time the call ended, he was starting the ignition of his Kia Picante. She pocketed her phone, comforted to know he'd soon be at the theater with her.

A moment later, Van parked his cruiser near the group and stepped out of the driver's seat. As Polly threw her arms around him, practically knocking him off his feet, a second cruiser pulled up. Detective Inspector Kerry McCormick, who worked out of the county headquarters, emerged from the vehicle on the passenger side. As usual, her sleek russet hair was arranged in a neat bun at the nape of her neck. Sergeant Adam Oduba, a young officer from Ghana, stepped out of the driver's seat.

Van returned Polly's hug then took a deep breath. Harriet hid a small smile as she witnessed the concerned husband transform into the professional police officer. He introduced DI McCormick and Sergeant Oduba to Joel then scanned the group. "I think you know everyone else."

Murmured greetings were exchanged, then the inspector took control. Along with Mateo Royan, the fire chief, who'd also arrived, she listened intently to Joel's description of the noise. To his dismay, she insisted he stay outside while she, Van, Chief Royan, and Sergeant Oduba took the precaution of clearing the building.

"After we rule out gunfire," DI McCormick explained, "we'll locate the source of the explosion."

Chief Royan instructed his firefighters to sweep the exterior.

As the emergency responders headed for the theater, Joel stuck his hands in his pockets, leaned against the fender of Van's cruiser, and hung his head.

Harriet prayed for Will's quick arrival, more for Joel's sake than her own. He desperately needed a friend right now. She had no idea what to say to him, but at least she could stand beside him. Before she'd taken a step, though, Andrew approached the cruiser. He said something to Joel, the words too quiet for anyone else to hear, then leaned against the fender beside him.

"Is Will on his way?" Kezia asked.

Harriet startled. She'd been so intent on watching Joel and Andrew that she hadn't heard Kezia approach.

"Sorry." Kezia smiled apologetically. "I didn't mean to frighten you."

"You're fine. I suppose we're all on edge."

"Joel definitely is. He thinks someone is purposely trying to sabotage him."

"Sabotage?" The knot in Harriet's stomach tightened. Was this the work of Dankworth, the guy from the diner who was talking about his great-uncle ruining plans? Assuming he was responsible, had he escalated his threatening behavior from writing intimidating letters to…what, exactly? Actually setting off a bomb in his competitor's theater when there were people inside?

Harriet could hardly endure the path her thoughts were taking her down.

"So Joel thinks someone did this on purpose?" she asked.

"I know it seems unlikely. But there've been so many unexplained things happening." Kezia shivered, and she wrapped her arms around herself.

"Such as the ghost?" Harriet asked in a low tone so that neither Polly nor Ruby could overhear her.

"I know what I saw." Kezia defiantly lifted her chin. "I also know it's not possible."

"What exactly did you see?"

"My stomach was feeling a little queasy, so I ducked out to the backstage loo."

"The one by the wardrobe room?" Harriet clarified.

Kezia nodded. "When I came out, I heard a noise from the other end of the corridor. The lighting was so dim, I couldn't see anything. Then, all of a sudden, this ethereal being emerged from the shadows." She paused then shook her head as if in disbelief. "I kid you not, Harriet. He looked like he stepped out of a Charles Dickens novel. He even wore a top hat."

Her cheeks pinked, and Harriet laid a comforting hand on her shoulder.

"It must've been someone's idea of a practical joke." She made a mental note to have Will talk to Joshua and Caleb.

Kezia dropped her arms and shifted her stance to better face Harriet. "At first I didn't want to tell anyone about the ghost because I was so embarrassed at how much it frightened me. Now I don't want to give whoever managed to pull off such a stunt any of the attention they so obviously crave."

"I'm sorry I told Polly," Harriet said. "And I told Will, and we both told Joel. Van knows too."

The knot in Harriet's stomach clenched even tighter. After that pathetic apology, Kezia would never want to be friends.

"I wasn't chastising you." Kezia pressed her lips together. "I'm chastising myself. If I'd said something sooner, demanded an explanation, maybe this"—she waved her arm toward the theater—"wouldn't have happened."

"You can't blame yourself. Besides, for all we know, the explosion was caused by some kind of mechanical failure." Harriet wasn't sure if she was trying to convince herself or Kezia.

"I hope that's the case. I hate to think anyone in White Church Bay could be so cruel." Kezia groaned. "It doesn't make sense that Joel would have an enemy here. The only person who even knew him before he moved here is Will, and we know he isn't writing ridiculous notes or setting off bombs."

"I assure you," Harriet said, unable to hide her amusement at the thought, "he is not." She tilted her head. "Wait a minute. You know about the notes?"

"Joel told Andrew and me when we were in the workroom." Kezia gestured toward the driveway. "Speaking of your shining knight, here he comes."

Harriet jogged to the Kia, and as soon as Will stepped out of his car, she melted into his arms and found herself strengthened by his comfort. While he held her, she brought him up to speed on what was happening. "DI McCormick is with Van. They're checking out the theater along with Chief Royan and Sergeant Oduba."

She also shared her concerns about Joel and the conversation she'd had with Kezia.

"Kezia makes a great point," Will said. "About no one here knowing Joel before he came. Joel insists he's never met Cyril Dankworth before or his great-uncle Egbert. Why would they or anyone else around here have a grudge against Joel?"

"Maybe someone knows him, but he doesn't know someone." Harriet laughed. "Does that make sense?"

Will squeezed her hand. "Enough that I know what you mean. Sad to say, Joel made plenty of enemies when he was younger."

"And yet God blessed him by giving him you to be his friend."

"A cautious friend who needs to be a better one."

Will was about to say something more when Polly shouted Harriet's name. As Van and DI McCormick strode across the drive toward Joel, Harriet and Will hurried to join them.

"The explosion came from the electrical room," the inspector said.

Andrew frowned. "In that case, I would have thought all the lights would have gone out and stayed out."

"I'm not an electrician, so I can't explain what caused the lights to flicker. Though I can say there's not as much damage as you'd expect from a noise as loud as the one you described." The inspector's facial expression gave nothing away, which caused Harriet to suspect she wasn't telling everything she knew.

"Doesn't sound like an accident to me," Andrew muttered.

DI McCormick ignored Andrew and focused her attention on Joel. "Chief Royan said you can go inside if you want, but he's shut off the power. You should have someone inspect the circuits before turning it back on."

"That's great." Joel blew out a frustrated breath, and his eyes reddened. "This kind of setback could ruin everything."

Will moved to stand beside his friend. "You go ahead and talk to the chief. I'll call Piers and see if he's available to come over and check out the system."

"I almost hope he isn't," Joel grumbled.

Will's brows drew together. "Do you want me to call someone else?"

"Don't mind me. This isn't one of my best days." With a pained smile, Joel placed his hand on Will's shoulder. "Thanks for being here, buddy. I don't know what I'd do without your support."

Will nodded then shot a glance in Harriet's direction. She could read his thoughts in his eyes—he still felt guilty for the lingering doubts he'd had about Joel.

Harriet responded to his glance with an encouraging smile. How much she loved this incredible man.

While Will called Piers Berrycloth, the contractor who'd overseen the theater's electrical and plumbing upgrades, Harriet took out her phone to call Martha. She'd hoped to be back at the farm over an hour ago.

Well-laid plans and all that.

When Martha answered, Harriet explained what had happened and that she'd be on her way after she stopped by the clinic.

"Come whenever you can," Martha said. "By the way, I found that autographed menu card I was telling you about and several other keepsakes you might like to see."

Harriet felt her spirits lift. "That's much-needed good news. I'll see you soon."

After a quick chat with Will and a see-you-later kiss, Harriet gave a brief statement to the officers and said her goodbyes to the others. For his part, Will had gotten ahold of Piers, who was now on his way to the theater. Will planned to stay with Joel and give him moral support for as long as he was needed. He and Van were heading into the building as Harriet backed out of her parking space.

Her thoughts were a jumbled mess as she picked up the items she wanted from the clinic, including what she now referred to as the Okehurst file—all the information she'd gathered on Eugenie and her mysterious disappearance—and drove to Martha's hobby farm.

She'd experienced a full range of emotions today, including a thrilling confidence that she *was* Elizabeth Bennet when she put on the gorgeous blue gown she'd selected. Then there was the fun of being pampered as a star with her name on a dressing room door and her very own vanity, and then the fright caused by the explosion.

She shared Andrew's skepticism and couldn't help wondering if there was more to the story than the tight-lipped inspector was telling.

Harriet laid the sedated cat on the scale, and Martha recorded the information on a medical records form. Thankfully, getting the Kellas cat to sleep had been a breeze. The crates in the isolation room were set up so that either a sedative or oxygen could be pumped into the animal's space.

"She's a healthy weight," Harriet said. "Someone's been taking care of her, or else she's a good hunter."

"I wish I knew which," Martha said. "I can't help wondering if she accidentally got into a live trap. But then I have to ask why whoever trapped her didn't simply release her."

"Maybe they didn't realize how feral she is." Harriet moved the cat to the examination table and went through her usual routine of listening to the heartbeat and lungs, taking her temperature, and checking her ears, nose, and mouth.

"No infections, no visible parasites," she said as Martha continued to take notes. "Her skin looks good. No lesions or any signs of being caught in a snare. That's good news."

"I asked Garth if he'd seen her on any of his game cameras." Martha shrugged. "Unfortunately, he hadn't."

Harriet understood Martha's frustration. If the cat had tripped one of the motion cameras that Garth had set up in the moors, then they could have pinpointed her territory and the optimal place to release her. Without knowing anything about the cat's history, Martha had a difficult decision to make. Releasing her into her native habitat was the preferred route to take, but right now they didn't know if she could survive on her own.

As Harriet's expert fingers checked the limp cat's abdomen, she suddenly froze.

"What's wrong?" Martha asked.

Harriet shifted the cat to her back and gently caressed her stomach. "She's pregnant. About four weeks along, I'd say."

"Oh my." Martha held the cat's giant black paw between her finger and thumb. "That does complicate matters, doesn't it?"

"I can arrange to do an ultrasound if you'd like me too. We'd have to take her to the clinic though."

Martha tilted her head then shook it. "We'll know her due date when labor begins, and we'll know the number of babies when they're born. Is there any reason to put her under such stress?"

"Nope," Harriet said. "In fact, I'd rather not sedate her again."

"She'll be comfortable in the Sanctuary Suite during her confinement. We can put her there when you're finished with the exam."

"That sounds perfect. As soon as she has a vitamin shot and her vaccinations, we'll get her settled."

While Harriet administered the shots, Martha left to prepare the room for its latest guest.

"Ready to see your new home, little mama?" Harriet murmured as she cradled the cat and carried her to a large stall that had been renovated into an enriched habitat.

The Kellas cat could be watched through the fine mesh that stretched from the top of the stall's wooden boards to the ceiling. Logs, planks, and cubbies provided opportunities to climb and hide. Martha turned on the shallow rock fountain so that fresh water bubbled up to create a plate-sized pool.

"I put a bed for her in here." Martha gestured to the hollow in the base of a faux tree. "She'll feel safe there."

Harriet gently placed the cat inside the hollow and covered her with a light blanket. "She'll be groggy when she wakes up."

"And hungry. Should I put food out for her now?"

"You might as well. She'll eat when she feels up to it." Harriet reviewed other instructions with Martha though it hardly seemed necessary, given the older woman's experiences with tending a variety of animals, both domestic and wild. "Do you mind if I stop in every few days to check on her?"

"Come whenever you like." Martha led the way out of the stall and latched the door behind them. "Give me a minute to set up the camera, and then we can go to the house and look at my memorabilia. And keep an eye on my newest guest."

As soon as the camera was set up, Harriet and Martha strolled along the lane to the farmhouse. Martha prepared tea while Harriet added notes to the cat's medical form.

"What name should I put down for her?" Harriet asked.

"The giving of names is such a heavy responsibility." Martha set a plate of homemade chocolate walnut cookies on the table along with a caddy of various teabags. "Even though I don't expect she'll stay here once her kittens are weaned, it seems disrespectful to call her 'the cat' for all that time."

"You'll have her about two-and-a-half months, give or take a few days."

After that? Most likely the kittens would be placed in rescue homes or sanctuaries—Martha had plenty of experience making those decisions—but Mama's fate wouldn't be so easily decided.

"I think I'll call her Hagar," Martha said. "How does that suit?"

"It's lovely." Harriet wrote the name at the top of the medical form then slid the clipboard into her veterinary bag.

Martha poured boiling water into their teacups then joined Harriet at the table. She took the lid off a stationery-sized box, smiled broadly, and held up the menu card.

"Eugenie's autograph," she said with pride. "I only wish it had been on her photo. But my husband and I didn't have one of those instant developing cameras then. Their popularity had waned. And we weren't carrying around phones that could take selfies then either."

She handed Harriet the menu card.

"Isn't her handwriting beautiful?" Martha said. "Cursive is a lost art these days. Children don't know how to form the letters, and many of them are unable to read a letter that isn't printed."

"Aunt Jinny says the same thing." Harriet studied the autograph. "I appreciate how legibly Eugenie writes her name. I've seen autographs that are nothing but a scrawl."

"Her *E* seems especially distinctive."

"I don't think I've ever seen one quite like it," Harriet said. She narrowed her eyes as she studied the capital letter. "But I should have."

"What do you mean?"

Harriet's heart raced as she retrieved the Okehurst file from the front pocket of her veterinary bag. "I brought a copy of the letter that Eugenie wrote to her friend after she eloped."

Martha's mouth formed an *O* as she leaned forward. Then she said, "May I read it?"

Instead of answering, Harriet placed Eugenie's handwritten letter next to Martha's autographed menu card and compared the signatures. Her stomach dropped to her feet as she turned the letter and the card so that Martha could see them.

"Are my eyes deceiving me?" she asked.

"Only if mine are deceiving me too." Martha stared at Harriet. "Eugenie didn't write that letter."

Text Thread
Saturday, October 11, 2025

WHAT IN THE WORLD WERE YOU THINKING?
  YOU COMPLAINING ABOUT SOMETHING?
  YOU'RE A FOOL WHO CAN'T TELL TIME.
  I DON'T KNOW WHAT YOU'RE TALKING ABOUT.
  THAT THING WENT OFF THIS AFTERNOON. THAT'S P.M. I SAID A.M.
  NOBODY WAS HURT. WHAT DOES IT MATTER?
  BECAUSE WHEN I TELL YOU TO DO SOMETHING, THAT'S WHAT YOU DO.

CHAPTER ELEVEN

Harriet could hardly focus on Will's sermon the next morning. Considering how little sleep they'd gotten the night before, she didn't know how he managed to exude such energy. She stifled a yawn and did her best to focus on his message, a last-minute substitution for the sermon he'd originally prepared.

He'd spent most of the evening in the furnished flat Joel rented above the Tales and Treasures bookshop. The corner building with its quaint bow-front windows was one of Harriet's favorites in the village. If she and Will ever downsized to a cozy one-bedroom apartment—not that she had any plans to do so—she'd love to live above the bookshop. How fun to be that close to so much imagination and creativity.

When Will finally arrived home, Harriet greeted him with the news that Polly and Van were on their way with pizza for a late supper and handed him a mug of hot chocolate with mini-marshmallows and peppermint flakes.

"Joel is completely wrecked," Will told her as he wrapped his hands around the mug. "First the threatening notes and rumors of the theater being haunted. Then to find out the explosion might not have been an accident? He thinks God is punishing him, and he's afraid his faith isn't strong enough to withstand the adversity."

Because of Joel's crisis of faith, Will had scrapped his prepared sermon and stayed up till the wee hours of the morning to craft a message about God's grace. "This sermon is for me too," he had said at breakfast. His inner struggle to accept his friend as a changed man still pained him. While he'd been with Joel the evening before, he'd once again asked for his forgiveness, and Joel had asked the same of Will.

Now, on this crisp autumn morning, Will stood in the three-tiered pulpit and preached to the parishioners sitting in their walled family boxes or on the balcony benches. His message focused on the importance of extending grace to others even—especially—when it was hard.

His delivery was compelling, yet Harriet's mind wandered once again. While devouring the delicious pizza the night before, Van had said little about the ongoing joint police/fire investigation into the explosion at the theater, though he quipped that the incident was a case of the bark being worse than the bite. The sound had reverberated throughout the theater, but the damage was mostly confined to the electrical room, the stairs leading to it, and the wall separating that area from the lobby. His reluctance to share any more details only confirmed Harriet's fear that the frightening explosion was no accident.

Their conversation had then switched to the Okehurst cold case. Martha had insisted that Harriet show her autographed menu card to Van so he could see for himself that Eugenie hadn't written the letter to Layla Hastings. He immediately agreed that the signatures didn't match and said he'd talk to DI McCormick about the case.

"I don't know that it'll make a difference," he said, his tone apologetic. "Even if the case gets reopened, it won't be a priority. Not until this latest situation gets sorted out."

Harriet knew enough about the workings of law enforcement to understand why a forty-year-old disappearance wasn't as important as what was happening in the here and now. But she really wanted to know if Eugenie had married the love of her life or was the victim of some nefarious scheme.

"It's so strange," Polly commented, "that an unsolved mystery from when the playhouse closed is vying for our attention with a mystery happening all these years later when the playhouse is opening again. And that the same play is being performed."

"At least *Pride and Prejudice* isn't a mystery too," Van joked.

"For now," Will said, "our primary concern is to help Joel any way we can."

Harriet had agreed. They needed to protect their friend until his enemy had been identified and exposed.

Since the explosion at the Beacon was officially under police investigation, Van would be devoting all his time to the case. A forty-year-old cold case, no matter how mysterious or sensational, would have to wait its turn.

Unless Harriet could ferret out a new lead.

As Will encouraged the congregation to share with others the grace promised to them by their heavenly Father, Harriet prayed for wisdom and guidance. Since she'd first heard about the missing Eugenie, she'd been fascinated by the actress's story. More importantly, she'd felt convinced that something wasn't quite right with the official explanation and that it was up to her to find out the truth.

To accomplish that goal, she needed to locate Layla and discover the identity of Eugenie's supposed groom. If he even existed.

She'd begin her personal investigation this afternoon doing her own internet searches. If she couldn't find anything, then she'd do her best to visit Colleen at the *Gazette* office one day this week. Hopefully, she'd be available to put her research skills to use to find out what happened to the seamstress.

Harriet was brought back to the present when Will concluded his message by asking the congregation to stand. "Let's all turn to our bulletins and read Colossians 3:13 together."

With one voice, the congregation read the verse. "'Bear with each other and forgive one another if any of you has a grievance against someone. Forgive as the Lord forgave you.'"

Will closed his Bible. "I urge you to memorize this verse if you haven't already hidden it in your heart. We'll close this morning's service by singing a classic hymn and one of my favorites, 'Amazing Grace.'"

The congregation raised their voices in song, then an elder said the closing prayer. "Go in peace," Will declared as the service came to an end.

Harriet gathered her Bible and purse then followed Polly and Van out of the boxed pew. She engaged in friendly conversations with one person after another as she made her way to the back of the church. A couple of Aunt Jinny's friends wanted to know when she'd be returning from her continental trip and asked how she was enjoying her vacation with her family.

Harriet sent her aunt a brief text most mornings and got one in return, but she hadn't attempted to text about Eugenie or Kezia's ghost or even the explosion. All those details would have to wait until Aunt Jinny's return.

By then, Harriet hoped to have more answers and fewer questions. Elena stopped her as she neared the end of the aisle. "I know this is last minute, but do you and Will have plans for lunch? Garth and I are taking Jack on a autumn picnic and want to invite you to come along."

"That sounds so fun," Harriet said, truly disappointed she couldn't say yes. But yesterday's circumstances had prevented Will from finishing his long to-do list. When Harriet volunteered to help him, he'd suggested she stay home to keep Maxwell, Charlie, and Ash company since they'd been left alone so much lately.

At her insistence, he'd finally given her a few items from his list that she could take care of from home. She planned to tackle them first, then she could focus on finding Layla and the mysterious groom. Meanwhile, with fewer obligations of his own to complete, Will would have time later in the day to help Joel clean up the debris from the explosion.

If all went well, they'd finally have their quiet evening at home.

Instead of saying all that, Harriet told Elena that Will had things to do for the bazaar. "Please ask us again. We love exploring the moors, and an autumn picnic is a terrific idea."

"We definitely will," Elena promised before she was pulled into a different conversation.

Harriet turned and almost bumped into Poppy.

"How serendipitous to run into you," Poppy exclaimed. "Have you decided what committee to join?"

Harriet wasn't sure how serendipitous it was for her and Poppy to meet in church after a Sunday service they both regularly attended, but there was no need to go down that rabbit trail. Not when she was about to burst Poppy's hopeful bubble.

"I'm sorry, Poppy. Truly I am. But with everything else going on, I haven't given it a thought. Will has given me a few things to do for him, and I'm sure I'll be helping Aunt Jinny when she returns."

"You didn't even look at the list?" A hurtful tone edged Poppy's voice.

"What list?"

"The one I emailed you. With all the committees and what they do and who chairs them."

Harriet inwardly groaned. "I haven't checked my email recently. I'm sorry."

Poppy released an incredibly heavy sigh. Harriet wasn't sure she'd ever seen her this upset before.

"I'll look at it this afternoon," Harriet promised. "I'll be home the rest of the day—"

"That's wonderful news." Poppy's eyes lit up. "You can drive to Skipton to pick up the spin-the-wheel board. I can't thank you enough for doing this, Harriet. I wasn't sure how to get the board today, but it's like God put you in my path as an answer to my prayer."

He did? God, can we talk about this?

"I'll call the rental store manager and let him know. This is so wonderful."

"But Skipton is almost two hours away."

"Don't you think I know it?" Poppy's huge smile almost split her pleasant features in half. "I've made that trip the past three years. But you're an American. I've heard Americans think nothing of driving several hours in a day. Besides, you're doing me such a big favor. I'll text you the address. Now you'll have to excuse me. I need to have a word with Ruby before she disappears out the door. Usually,

I can count on her help in so many areas. But this year, she's spending entirely too much time at the theater on all those costumes. Like so many others."

To Harriet's surprise, Poppy actually tut-tutted as she maneuvered her way through the crowd.

"I'm so sorry," Polly whispered as she moved closer to Harriet. "I'd volunteer to go for you, but the children's games committee is meeting this afternoon."

"It's okay." Harriet forced a smile—she never knew who might be watching the new pastor's wife with a critical eye—and inwardly let go of her afternoon plans. So much for spending time with the Bailey-Knight menagerie and giving Will a hand with his to-do list. A quiet evening was probably out of the question. "Maybe I'm meant to take this trip for some reason. And maybe, if I do this major thing, Poppy will give me grace the next time I say no."

"Like in Will's sermon," Polly suggested as they went to join their husbands.

"Since you had to bring that up," Harriet said, half-joking, "I suppose I need to extend *her* grace."

Polly shot Harriet an impish grin. "You can do it."

She could and she would. Meanwhile, the search for Layla and the missing groom was only postponed by a few hours. A day or two at most.

After a quick lunch at home, Harriet and Will went their separate ways—Will to the church and Harriet, with Maxwell going along for the ride, to Skipton. Harriet had removed his prosthetic wheels and clipped the doggy car seat strap to his harness so he was safe, secure, and comfortable.

Her interaction with the rental manager was brief. As soon as the huge spinning wheel board was secured in the back of the Beast, she texted Poppy to let her know she was on her way to the church.

Poppy's reply came after Harriet had been driving at least half an hour. She waited until she reached a rural crossroads to stop and read it.

If I'm not at the church when you get there, give me a call.

Harriet refrained from rolling her eyes and responded with a smiley face then went back to listening to one of her favorite historical podcasts. The hosts' soothing voices as they discussed palace intrigues from centuries ago along with the drive on country roads lined with hedges and vistas of pastures made the time go fast and the trip a pleasant one.

When Harriet finally arrived at the church, she parked beside Poppy's vehicle. "At least she's still here." Harriet rubbed Maxwell's head. "Soon we'll be home, and then Will will be home, and we'll all have a nice quiet evening together."

They'd already agreed to set aside the bazaar to-do lists and even Harriet's research plans. Tonight, their priority would be each other.

Harriet texted Poppy to let her know she was in the parking lot. "I'm not leaving you," she said to Maxwell when she opened her door. He cocked his head as if he understood then rested his long muzzle on the car seat's padded side.

As Harriet opened the trunk, Poppy burst through the church's side doors and scurried to her.

"This is wonderful," she said, a huge smile on her face as she clasped her hands together. "Thank you so much for making the trip. You didn't mind too much, did you?"

"Not at all." As she said the words, Harriet realized she meant them. She'd spent time with Maxwell and allowed herself to get lost in the distant past instead of fixating on a forty-year-old elopement. Maybe bumping into Poppy—or Poppy bumping into Harriet—really had been God-directed serendipity.

Harriet removed the blanket covering the spin-the-wheel board and started to pull it out of the hatch.

"Stop," Poppy cried, a look of horror erasing the smile. "What is this?"

"It's the spin-the-wheel board. What you told me to get."

"No, no, no. This can't be right. It's entirely unsuitable."

"What's wrong with it?"

"We needed the one with numbers, not the one with colors. You'll have to take it back."

"Now?" Harriet blurted, her tone incredulous.

Poppy glanced at her watch. "I guess it is too late to make that drive again today. What about tomorrow?"

Harriet stared at Poppy, whose eyes shimmered with hope while the lines around her mouth were tight with worry.

"It's just," Poppy said, pulling her sweater closer against the chill of the breezes blowing inland from the sea, "I'd hate for the church to pay rental fees on something we can't use."

"I can't be gone from the clinic that long. Not tomorrow or any other day this week."

"You're busy," Poppy admitted. "But someone needs to do something about this mix-up. And I have too many other details to tend to."

Before Harriet could respond, Poppy scurried into the warmth of the church.

Frustrated over what seemed like—scratch that—what definitely *was* an ungrateful dismissal, Harriet closed the hatch and drove home. Her mood immediately brightened at seeing Will's Kia parked in its usual spot. Their quiet evening at home was about to become a reality.

She'd explain everything to Will over dinner and, between them, they'd figure something out. For now, though, she looked forward to an enjoyable dinner and conversation with her favorite person in the entire world.

Hours later, Harriet's buzzing phone awakened her to a frantic phone call from Mitchell Douglas, the owner of a gorgeous wolf sable Pomeranian with serious health issues.

"It's Beau." Mitch's voice cracked. "He's in a lot of pain."

CHAPTER TWELVE

When Mitch first arrived at Cobble Hill Clinic, he told Harriet that Beau experienced a frightening seizure in the midafternoon and had started limping afterward. Since he'd overheard Poppy's conversation with Harriet at church, he knew she was on her way to Skipton, so he'd taken Beau to an emergency veterinarian clinic.

An inexperienced vet tech there had given a cursory examination of Beau's leg and told Mitch to take him home and keep him quiet for a few days.

Beau seemed to do pretty well after Mitch took him home from the emergency clinic. But around midnight, he'd started whining and wouldn't let Mitch touch the leg. Because of Beau's age and neurological problems, Harriet assured Mitch he'd done the right thing by calling her.

Harriet x-rayed Beau's leg and wasn't surprised to see it was fractured. She sedated the little dog and set the bone then wrapped his leg in a cast.

After glancing at the clock, she sighed. For the second night in a row, sleep had been more of a dream than a reality. And here she was, at two o'clock on a Monday morning, wide awake and alert thanks to an adrenaline rush and a strong cup of coffee.

"How's he doing?" Mitch's words wavered with dread and exhaustion.

"He's endured much worse," she said. "I've put a cast on him, and I'll give you medication to ease his pain." She sat down in the chair beside him. "I'll keep him here tonight, but because of his age and more frequent seizures, I'd like you to take him to Castle View Veterinary Hospital in York to have them run some tests on him."

Though she was a skilled and competent surgeon, Harriet's small clinic wasn't equipped to run the kinds of tests Beau needed. "I can have Polly call first thing in the morning to make the appointment so you won't have to worry about doing that," she said.

Mitch nodded his agreement. Having been to the York animal hospital on multiple occasions, he was well aware of their superior resources.

"I wish I could take away his pain." Mitch took in a deep breath then slowly let it out. "Sometimes I think I'm selfish to be holding on to him like I do. But letting him go is too hard."

"I know it is." Harriet stroked the Pom's furry head. The delightful little guy was a lovable and forgiving fighter. In Mitch's shoes, she'd have the same struggle.

They'd had this difficult conversation twice now, when Beau's quality of life seemed barely existent. Mitch's decision was made more complicated because Beau had belonged to Mitch's twin brother, a British military officer who'd been killed by an IED in Afghanistan.

Though Mitch never said so, Harriet intuited that losing Beau would be like losing his brother all over again.

Both times when Mitch was on the verge of scheduling the dreaded appointment, Beau rallied in what could only be described as a miracle. For a few more months, until the next frightening attack, he enjoyed the luxurious life of a pampered pet.

Incidents such as this one compelled Mitch to once again face the question of whether the time had come to let Beau go.

"You should go home and get some rest," Harriet urged.

"What if he has another seizure? If he doesn't make it through the night..." Mitch averted his gaze.

"I'll be monitoring him," Harriet assured him. "If there's any change, I promise I'll call."

Mitch ran his hand through Beau's thick coat. "It's always hard to leave him."

Harriet didn't reply. Grandad had taught her that silence could be a helpful tonic for a patient's owner who needed time to control heartrending emotions. She'd allow Mitch a few more minutes before moving Beau to one of the nearby recovery kennels.

Mitch leaned over Beau to whisper in his ear. "I'll be back in a few hours, buddy. All I ask is that you wait for me." The Pom flicked his tongue over Mitch's chin.

Harriet's throat tightened, and she momentarily closed her burning eyes. She could usually stay dispassionately compassionate during moments like this one. Pet owners and their beloved animals deserved a veterinarian who behaved with professionalism, not a basket case who couldn't control her own emotions.

But the poignancy of Mitch's farewell, no doubt amplified by Harriet's lack of sleep, gripped her heart. She wished she could brandish a magic wand and transform Beau into the dog he'd been before his first seizure sent him along this road of blood tests, X-rays, and surgeries. That she could restore Mitch's brother to him.

But none of that was within her power. Job 13:15, which Harriet had memorized from the King James Version, came to her mind.

"*Though He slay me, yet will I trust in Him.*"

This side of heaven, neither she nor Mitch could understand God's purposes. But she could give thanks He'd given her the skill to give Mitch more time—perhaps hours, perhaps weeks—with the dog who meant so much to him.

Mitch rubbed his eyes as he straightened. "Thanks for, well, everything. I don't know what I would have done if you hadn't answered your phone tonight." He averted his gaze as he drew in a deep breath.

"I'm going to put him to bed now." Harriet carefully lifted Beau from the operating table and carried him to the recovery kennel she'd prepared for him. "Go to sleep now, little man." Beau responded with a tiny whimper then closed his eyes.

As she latched the door, Will came into the room.

"Am I interrupting?" he asked.

Harriet greeted him with a smile. "Not at all. Our patient is resting peacefully."

"That's good." Will shifted his gaze to Mitch. "The kettle's on in the kitchen. Could you use a cuppa?"

"Thanks, but I should get home. The sun will be up before we know it, though I don't expect I'll get much sleep tonight."

"I can fix you a cup to go," Will offered. "Or coffee, if you'd rather."

The corner of Mitch's mouth quirked up. "Coffee might be good. If you're sure it's not a bother."

"A bother to put a pod in a brewing machine? It's the simplest thing in the world." Will slung his arm around Mitch's shoulder and led him from the room.

"Thanks, Will," Harriet murmured as the two men disappeared through the door leading into the kitchen. She needed a few moments of Grandad's quiet tonic herself, and she appreciated Will giving them to her. As she considered what had happened to Beau, she tidied the surgery and disinfected the operating area.

With all her heart, Harriet wished she'd refused Poppy's request—no, her insistence—that she go get the spin-the-wheel board. Then she would've been home when Beau needed her. She could have set the bone hours ago and saved him unnecessary pain. Then he wouldn't have needed an emergency procedure in the wee hours of the morning that put his already ill health in more jeopardy.

She'd been needed here, available to do her job, a multitude of times more than she needed to drive to Skipton.

Especially since it turned out the entire errand had been for nothing. Part of her wished she'd responded with a snappy retort to Poppy's assumption that she'd drive to Skipton again. The fact she didn't was probably the work of her guardian angel helping her mind her tongue. As upset as she was with Poppy—and with herself—she didn't want to say something she'd later regret.

As Harriet recorded her notes on Beau's medical chart, Will came through the kitchen door, carrying a bulky inflatable air mattress.

Despite her exhaustion and troubled thoughts, Harriet grinned at him. "I've never seen that before. Where did it come from?"

"I've been hiding it until such a time as this." He unfolded the bed along a row of cabinets and plugged in the compressor. "I always knew that sooner or later we'd be pulling an all-nighter so you could keep an eye on a sick animal. It's not like this is the first time. But this mattress is bound to be more comfortable than a cot or a chair. We might even get an hour or two of sleep."

"What about Mitch? Did you leave him in the kitchen?"

"He's on his way home with a cup of strong coffee to keep him company. But I expect he'll be back at daybreak."

"I wouldn't be surprised. That little dog means the world to him."

Will drew Harriet into a comforting embrace. "And you mean the world to me."

CHAPTER THIRTEEN

To Harriet's surprise, Mitch wasn't standing outside the clinic door when she unlocked it a few hours later. Instead, he called for an update while she was reviewing the medical folders for the morning appointments. Since Polly was in the surgery area with Beau, Harriet answered the phone and was grateful she had good news to share.

"He had a peaceful night," she told Mitch as she sat in Polly's chair, "and went for a short walk this morning. He's alert, and his vital signs are promising."

Mitch's relieved sigh sounded through the phone. "That's what I hoped to hear. But not what I expected."

"Beau's a fighter. He's proven that again and again."

"He sure has," Mitch said, a hint of pride in his tone. "Was Polly able to get him an appointment?"

"She called first thing," Harriet replied. "The Castle View team is expecting you whenever you can get there."

"Tell her thanks for me. And thanks to you and Will for all you do too. See you soon."

Harriet smiled to herself as the call ended then rested her elbows on the desk and rubbed her temples. Will had insisted she try to sleep and he would stay awake and keep an eye on Beau. She'd tried, truly she had. But twice she'd awakened from a fitful sleep disturbed by fading dreams.

Her frustration with Poppy had subsided, only to be replaced by an inner conflict that gnawed at her stomach. As much as she wanted to be the perfect pastor's wife, she had an obligation to her veterinary practice. Her first duty was to make herself available to her clients and their furry family members.

Hearing footsteps coming from the hall, Harriet rose from the desk. She pretended to shuffle through the day's medical folders as Polly entered the waiting area.

"I just got off the phone with Mitch," Harriet told her. "He's on his way."

Polly rounded the desk and took her seat. "Is he going to take Beau to Castle View?"

"Straightaway. He thanks you for making the call."

"That's the least I could do for our little sweetheart." Polly tapped the spacebar on her computer, and the screensaver on her monitor switched to a series of apps neatly organized in multiple rows. "It's a shame he had to go through what he did last night."

Harriet studied the folder for her next patient even though she knew the medical history by heart. People make mistakes—she made mistakes—but the vet tech should have been more careful. An *emergency* vet, especially, should have taken the extra time and effort to x-ray Beau's leg.

Realizing her thoughts were descending into a whirlpool, Harriet froze then bit her lower lip. The reception area seemed unusually quiet, and she could sense Polly's eyes on her. Unable to meet her best friend's gaze after thinking such critical thoughts,

Harriet focused on relaxing the tension in her fingers and in her shoulders.

The emergency clinic wasn't blameless—whoever it was needed to know what had happened to Beau so they wouldn't make a similar mistake in the future—but Harriet knew, deep inside, that the careless vet was a mere scapegoat for her frustration. The true target for all the pent-up resentment bubbling inside her was the person staring back at her when she'd applied mascara that morning.

"What if," Polly said, her soft voice brushing against the silence, "instead of driving to Skipton yesterday, you and Will had gone to that Camelot Pub in Richmond you visited last year? Or spent the afternoon at the abbey ruins? Even if Mitch had called you when Beau had his seizure, you would have been too far away to help. He'd have needed to wait for you to return or take Beau to another vet."

"Which is what he did."

"Because that was his best and only choice. But here's what I want to know. If you'd been having fun with Will, or even on a road trip with me or Jinny or Elena, would you be blaming yourself now for what happened to Beau?"

"Maybe," Harriet retorted. Then she frowned. Nothing like turning into a four-year-old in front of her closest friend. Besides, Polly's question couldn't be so easily dismissed. "Probably not," she admitted.

Polly's sympathetic expression eased into a conspiratorial smile. "Poppy didn't need to be so bossy though. She can be the sweetest person except when it comes to the autumn bazaar. Then she turns into a tyrant."

"You don't know the rest of the story." Harriet shared Poppy's reaction when she saw the spin-the-wheel board. "It's still in the back of the Beast. Apparently, it's my responsibility to see it's returned."

"How can you possibly do that with your schedule?" Polly's indignant tone made Harriet smile.

"Will said we'd think of something."

"As long as you don't decide to make that drive again. If Poppy tries to guilt you into doing that, I'll just have to give her a piece of my mind."

Harriet's smile broadened, though she knew Polly probably wouldn't do any such thing. Even so, she appreciated her friend's fervent support. "What would I do without you?"

"You'd have an unorganized filing system and clients who owe you money."

"There's a smidgen of truth to that."

"A smidgen?" Polly humphed, but her eyes sparkled. "I'd say at least an imperial ton. And, for the American in the room, that's heavier than your ton."

Harriet chuckled as she recalled her first days at the clinic. She'd quickly learned how particular Polly was about her filing system. Her knowledge of the patients and their medical histories was outstanding and a great help to Harriet when she first took over the practice.

Harriet knew there was no one more competent to handle the bookkeeping and accounting than Polly. She was immensely grateful that she could completely depend on her to make sure the invoices got sent to clients and the clinic's bills got paid in a timely manner.

"The day begins," Polly announced in a singsong voice as she looked toward the glassed entrance. "Our first client is getting out of his car."

Harriet sorted through the medical folders till she found the one she needed then offered Polly a sheepish grin.

"You may need to organize these again." She pushed the remaining folders toward her.

"You didn't."

"I did."

Polly arched her eyebrow. "Told you."

The morning, thankfully, didn't have any hiccups even though Harriet drank more coffee than usual to fend off the yawns. Because of Saturday's explosion, Joel had canceled rehearsals for this evening, which meant both she and Will were free of any other commitments. She looked forward to a peaceful evening, a long relaxing bath, and an early bedtime.

When Mitch arrived, Polly gave him a printed copy of the notes detailing Beau's procedure for the Castle View Veterinary Hospital specialists while Harriet prepared the dog for the long car ride.

"If they have any questions or if you need anything, just call," she said to Mitch.

"And be sure to let us know what they say," Polly added.

"I doubt there'll be any miraculous breakthroughs," Mitch replied. "I'm praying the news isn't awful."

"We're praying for that too," Harriet assured him.

Once he'd gone, she said a silent prayer for him then returned to doing what she did best—taking care of God's creatures.

During their lunch break, Polly drove to the police station to have lunch with Van. After she left, Harriet stepped down the hallway from the clinic into her kitchen.

First, she popped a leftover casserole into the oven to reheat. Then she bundled Maxwell into a thick sweater with Velcro fasteners and headed outside for a brisk walk. Charlie and Ash were also shooed outdoors, though neither of them particularly wanted to go. Harriet couldn't blame them. The wind gusts seemed stronger and colder than they'd been over the weekend. Snowfall was a possibility, though so far none of the weather reports had it in their immediate forecast.

Once they were back inside the warm and cozy kitchen, Harriet settled at the island with her meal and her laptop. She planned to make use of the short amount of time she had to browse the internet.

She found nothing suitable when she searched for *Layla Hastings*—the few results were for women in their twenties and thirties—or for *Eugenie Okehurst*. Not that she'd expected to strike gold with the latter. If Colleen couldn't find anything, then Harriet certainly wouldn't.

On a whim, she searched *Beacon-on-the-Moor* and scrolled through the results. On the second page, a listing caught her eye that set her insides tingling like crazy.

PROMINENT RESIDENT INJURED IN TRAGIC FALL
From The Whitby Gazette
Wednesday, October 9, 1985
By Nancy Lennox

The unimaginable occurred at around nine o'clock Friday night, October 4, at the Beacon-on-the-Moor Playhouse during the opening night performance of the Stanhope Players' production of Pride and Prejudice.

Mr. Silas D. Hornsby, age twenty-four, who was enjoying the last few minutes of the second act, endured a tragic accident. As Lydia and Wickham raced off to Gretna Green, Mr. Hornsby tumbled from his private upper-level box onto the surprised theatergoers seated below.

Even though several days have passed in which the police have talked to witnesses, including Mr. Hornsby's guests for the evening, and conducted a thorough examination of the scene, the details surrounding Mr. Hornsby's drop to the floor below remain sketchy.

Investigators now know that three theatergoers who had the misfortune of sitting in the ill-fated section of the lower auditorium were struck by a piece of the upper box's wooden railing.

As Mr. Hornsby was immediately taken to the hospital and has yet to regain consciousness, investigators haven't been able to ask him any questions about the terrible tragedy. Officials speculate that Mr. Hornsby, in his exuberant enjoyment of the scene, may have leaned against the railing, which then gave way—though here it must be said that Mr. Hornsby is not an obese man but is said to have an admirable physique.

Until Mr. Hornsby is able to speak to us, we may never know what precipitated his fall.

One theory that investigators insist they do not accept as plausible involves the Top Hat Ghost, the specter who supposedly haunts the theater. Let it be unequivocally stated that sightings of the well-dressed ghost are rarely reported. Our local police officers are too level-headed to entertain such nonsense, and, for that, the good people of White Church Bay are grateful.

In addition to his head injuries, Mr. Hornsby's left leg and right arm were broken. He also suffered additional contusions and scrapes. Those hit by Mr. Hornsby or the balcony railing suffered a variety of injuries, with the most severe being that of Mrs. Claudia Witherspoon, who suffered a concussion and was kept in hospital overnight for observation. She is now resting comfortably at home with her family while she continues to recuperate from her harrowing experience.

Be sure to get your copy of next Wednesday's edition of The Whitby Gazette so you won't miss any updates to this developing story.

Harriet, whose meal remained untouched, leaned against the padded back of the island's stool.

"Wow," she said aloud. From his nearby bed, Maxwell raised his head from his paws to stare at her with his intelligent brown eyes.

"Just...wow," she repeated.

Why had no one mentioned this story when talking about the theater's past? Perhaps because the Mystery of the Missing Actress was much more compelling than Mr. Silas Hornsby's strange fall.

Then Harriet suddenly remembered what Malachi Atkins had said about getting seats in the center section of the theater's auditorium. If not for the phone call interrupting him, he may have shared more details about the incident. Though maybe not, since the dramatic Nancy Lennox—whose writing style Harriet now found more enlightening than ridiculous—had written that no one could say why or how he fell.

When Joel purchased the theater, the doors leading to the mezzanine level where the boxes were located had been fitted with new locks so no one could access them. He'd said the area was unsafe. Since one person had already fallen—probably because the eighteenth-century wood had rotted—he had good reason to fear someone else might fall too.

After taking a few bites of her meal, Harriet sent the article to the printer so she'd have a hard copy. Next, she searched for the story that was to appear in the next week's edition of the paper but couldn't find it in the results.

She searched for Silas Hornsby's name, but she found no more articles mentioning him that appeared in the *Gazette*.

Next, she used the reporter's name as her search term. Nancy Lennox had written multiple articles for the newspaper over a span of about ten years, but none of those had anything to do with Silas Hornsby's accident or his recovery.

Since that seemed strange, Harriet assumed that only certain articles from the *Gazette*'s archives had been published to the internet. Maybe she'd find the missing articles in the newspaper's online archives. She paid a small fee on the *Gazette*'s website to access the archives database. Within a few seconds, she found the October 9 article she'd already read. But a follow-up article wasn't to be found in subsequent editions of the newspaper.

"Except for that one article, it's like the accident never happened," she said to Maxwell. Unlike before, his long nose stayed on his crossed paws. "I get it. You're no longer interested in the fate of Mr. Silas Hornsby. What about Eugenie Okehurst?"

For the next fifteen minutes or so, Harriet searched the *Gazette* archives for anything she could find on the playhouse, the injured theatergoer, and the actress. But she either found information she already knew or that wasn't pertinent.

She scanned the October 9 article one more time then dialed Polly's cell phone.

"Am I late?" Polly asked. "I thought I was doing okay with time."

"You're fine," Harriet assured her. "By any chance, are you still at the police station?"

"Do you need to talk to Van? He's right here."

"I'd like to talk to you both. That is, if no one else is there."

"I love secrets," Polly enthused. "Okay, I'm putting you on speaker."

After returning Van's greeting, Harriet summarized the *Gazette* article she'd read about Silas Hornsby's accident at the Beacon.

"The strange thing is, I can't find any follow-up stories online or in the *Gazette*'s online archives. Polly, would you be willing to see what you can find in the physical archives? I'm sure Colleen will help you. I can handle things here at the clinic on my own for a while."

"I'd be glad too," Polly said. "It'll be like a scavenger hunt."

"Hopefully you'll find something helpful." Harriet paused and took a deep breath. "I need to ask you a favor too, Van."

"Does the favor involve me going into the vault?"

"How'd you guess?"

"As soon as you started talking about the investigation into the Hornsby accident, I looked it up on the database and found the evidence records number. If I thought of doing that, it was a given you'd thought of it too." Van chuckled. "You're our own Miss Marple—only half her age and not as arrogant."

"You think Miss Marple is arrogant?" Polly's are-you-kidding-me tone indicated her obvious disagreement. "She's smart and sweet and kind and a dear old soul."

"She's a busybody."

"Who solves every murder with her keen intellect and observation skills."

Harriet couldn't help grinning at the newlyweds' good-natured bickering. "I have a patient due in a few minutes, so you two will have to settle this disagreement without me."

She ended the call after thanking them for their help and hurried to tidy the kitchen before returning to the clinic. How she wished she could spend the afternoon looking at the evidence from the Beacon investigation and searching the *Gazette* archives with Colleen. Instead, she needed to trade her metaphorical detective deerstalker cap for her literal veterinarian smock.

At least she could count on Van and Polly to make copies of anything they found that was important. She would add those to her Okehurst file. Which should probably be renamed the Beacon-on-the-Moor file. After all, the Hornsby accident happened only a couple weeks before Eugenie Okehurst's disappearance.

"I hope she found true love," Harriet said to Maxwell. "That wherever she is and whoever she married, they made a beautiful life together."

Maxwell expressed his agreement with a joyous yip.

"And that Silas Hornsby made a full and complete recovery and attended many more plays where his 'admirable physique' did *not* fall from the balcony."

The dachshund's double yip caused Harriet to laugh.

As she returned to the clinic, however, pebbles of dread piled up in her stomach. That accident was a singular event. It made no sense that there wouldn't have been any follow-up stories about Silas's injuries or the reason the railing broke.

Unless something even stranger than the fall itself had happened behind the scenes.

CHAPTER FOURTEEN

In between appointments and waiting for Polly to return, Harriet sat at the desk in her grandfather's study to make a few follow-up calls. Even though he'd been gone almost two years now, she still thought of the very masculine room with its wall-lined bookshelves, heavy furniture, and leather chairs as Grandad's instead of hers.

One wall displayed several of Harold Bailey's original works of art. Outside of Yorkshire he was recognized as a famous artist and his oil paintings of landscapes and animals were valued by collectors and the general public. Visitors flocked to the art gallery, located in a stone outbuilding with a thatched roof on the Cobble Hill Farm property. To the locals, however, Old Doc Bailey had been a beloved vet who painted rather than a talented artist who cared for animals.

Like the kitchen, the study also had a door that led into the clinic. Harriet appreciated that she could slip in there whenever she wanted to look something up in one of Grandad's reference books or when she needed a moment or two to pull herself together after an especially difficult appointment.

At those times, she especially felt his presence. And that was the sole reason she'd made so few changes to the room. A couple of plants, a framed wedding photo of her and Will next to a favorite photo of her with her grandfather, and a well-loved stuffed bunny from her childhood on a shelf behind the desk were about the only additions she'd made to the study she'd inherited.

Harriet took a sip of her cinnamon spice tea and opened the top folder on her stack. One by one she made calls to a few of the farmers whose ewes and rams she'd cleared for tupping season. No one seemed to have any concerns, though Mrs. Atkins, who'd answered the phone, said how much she'd appreciated Will's sermon the day before.

"That verse we said at the end is one I've said to myself more times than I want to admit," she continued. "Funny how the verse convicts me to think of someone other than myself and also brings me comfort at the same time."

Harriet grimaced inside. As much as she tried to be objective and sensible about yesterday's events, she still couldn't think of Poppy without a heaping teaspoon of resentment bubbling up inside her. She wasn't being fair—she knew that—but the irritation wouldn't go away.

"You already had the verse hidden in your heart then?" Harriet asked.

"Since I was a newly married lass and discovered Mr. Atkins wasn't perfect. You can't believe how many times I repeated that scripture to myself to keep from saying something ugly out loud." She chuckled. "And it worked. Over our many years together, those annoying habits of his either disappeared or became endearing."

After the call ended, Harriet looked up Colossians 3:13 on her Bible app then copied it onto an index card so she could hide it in her heart too.

"Bear with each other," she murmured. Funny how the forgiveness didn't seem as difficult as the bearing. Polly was right when she said Harriet's guilt over not being available for Beau wouldn't have been as acute if she'd been out-of-town for any other reason. Which meant her irritation had more to do with her feelings about Poppy than the errand itself.

She'd been blindsided, had her expectations for her Sunday afternoon upended, and let her insecurities get the best of her. But what if she put herself in Poppy's shoes?

Though Harriet hoped she'd have been more diplomatic, she had to admit it wouldn't be easy to find someone willing to run that errand. As Poppy had indicated, the British had a much different view of time and distance than Americans. To make a two-hour drive in one day was practically anathema. Even more so when it ended up being a four-hour round trip.

As the organizer of this year's autumn bazaar, Poppy was bearing the enormous responsibility of making sure the event was a success. Harriet needed to keep that in mind when—if—her frustration returned. Though it still would have been nice for Poppy to ask instead of saying "do this" and running off before Harriet could respond.

"Bear with each other," she repeated. She was immediately reminded of the biblical counsel to bear one another's burdens. That was what she'd done yesterday, and Poppy's lack of gratitude couldn't change that simple fact.

Needing to get back to work, Harriet set aside the index card and opened the final folder in her stack. Martha Banks answered the call with a cheery hello and good news. "Hagar is skittish when I stop by to see her," she reported, "but she's not as feral as we thought. When I spy on her, she's either napping or enjoying the warmth from a patch of sunlight. This morning, I caught her batting around one of her toys and pouncing like a kitten."

"That sounds promising," Harriet said. "And such welcome news especially with babies coming." Based on the research she'd done, Harriet doubted Hagar would ever lose her feral spirit. Even Kellas kittens born in captivity rarely became domesticated house pets. The best option was to place them with rural farmers where they could roam free and still have someone make sure they had food and shelter available to them.

When all the calls were completed, Harriet returned to the clinic and checked her email. The emergency veterinarian, in response to her request, had sent a short message and attached Beau's record from his Sunday visit there. After a few moments to gather her thoughts, Harriet composed a gently worded email addressing the aftermath of Beau's visit.

As she hit the send button, Polly breezed in. "The wind is picking up. There's a storm brewing, or I wasn't born and raised beside the sea."

"I don't think I'd mind a good storm." Harriet practically shivered with delight at the thought. "A bowl of hearty stew with freshly baked bread. A roaring fire in the fireplace. That mystery I've been longing to read. What could be better?"

"Please invite me. I'm at the boy-loses-girl phase in the romance I'm reading and can't wait to find out if he wins her back." Polly shrugged out of her coat and hung it on the nearby rack.

"You know he will. They always do." Harriet pushed away from the desk so Polly could reclaim her seat.

"It's not so much the *if*," Polly retorted with a pretend haughty air. "It's the *how*. I'd love to spend the evening finding out while a storm rages outside. Meanwhile, Colleen says hello and she's sorry these searches are so unhelpful."

Harriet's heart sank. "She didn't find anything?"

"Nothing promising came up when she searched for Layla Hastings. The online archives weren't much help either, so she took me down to their storage area." Polly tucked her bag in its usual spot in the bottom desk drawer after removing a folded piece of paper. "Though their archives are a much better place to search for old stuff than Van's vault."

Harriet couldn't hide her curiosity and saw no reason to try. She pointed at the paper. "What's that?"

"We found the article about Silas Hornsby's accident," Polly said, ignoring Harriet's question. "And we found the newspaper that came out the following week. Colleen and I both went through it, page by page, and there was absolutely nothing more said about the accident. So we looked at the week after that and the week after that and the week after that."

"Polly!"

Her impish grin faded, and her eyes grew serious as she slid the paper over to Harriet. "That's when we found this. Colleen said it should have been in the online archives. She found it very odd that it wasn't."

Even more curious than before, Harriet unfolded the sheet of paper and found an enlarged photocopy of an obituary notice. Beside the text was a grainy black-and-white photo of a young man with handsome features and light-colored hair and eyes.

OBITUARIES
November 6, 1985
Silas D. Hornsby

Silas Hornsby, the only son of Lucas and Delphinia Hornsby, both deceased, is now reunited with his parents in

Paradise. As regular readers of this newspaper are aware, Mr. Hornsby, twenty-four, suffered a tragic fall attending a performance of Jane Austen's esteemed classic Pride and Prejudice *at the Beacon-on-the-Moor Playhouse located near the quaint village of White Church Bay a few short weeks ago.*

On the evening of Friday, October 4, he was enjoying the performance, seated in his reserved box on the theatre's mezzanine level. Suddenly, Mr. Hornsby broke through the balcony railing and landed upon those seated in the auditorium below.

Due to his severe injuries, Mr. Hornsby spent his final days in the York Community Hospital. His doctors were optimistic that, in time, Mr. Hornsby would make a full recovery, but, alas, fate had other plans. The unfortunate young man, who was often referred to as Yorkshire's most eligible bachelor, fell asleep one night and did not awaken the next morning.

Mr. Hornsby's funeral will be held at White Church, White Church Bay, on Thursday, November 7, at noon. His remains will be laid to rest in the church's historic graveyard.

When Harriet finished, she stared at Polly. "I have never read an obituary quite like that one."

"It's a literary masterpiece," Polly exclaimed. "I know it's sad and tragic that Silas died, but his obituary is like a short story. Full of drama and mystery and even romance. Can you imagine the heartbreak when Yorkshire's most eligible bachelor died after falling from a balcony?" Polly clutched her hands to her heart and struck a pose.

"A short story with a lot of missing pieces. It doesn't give his cause of death. Or even the exact date he died." Harriet skimmed the paper again. "Were all the obituaries in the *Gazette* like this one?"

"Colleen said the obituary writer at that time was the owner's widowed aunt," Polly explained. "She needed a little bit of income so she could stay in the house she'd lived in all her life, but she wasn't one to take charity. So the owner paid her to write the obituaries and the occasional article."

"That also sounds like the nugget of a short story," Harriet mused. "Maybe even a novel."

Polly chuckled. "A collection of her obituaries might be entertaining. Maybe I should suggest it to Colleen."

The ringing of the clinic's phone ended the conversation. While Polly slid into professional mode and answered the call, Harriet returned to Grandad's study, where she'd left her Beacon/Okehurst folder.

The tone of the obituary was so similar to that of the newspaper article about Silas's fall that Harriet couldn't help wondering if the widowed aunt had written both pieces. Was she the dramatic Nancy Lennox?

Harriet placed the obituary in the folder then knelt down to give Maxwell a cuddle. "Silas Hornsby's unexpected death is another mystery to pile on top of all the other mysteries occupying my thoughts," she said. "And perhaps the one with the easiest solution." An undetected and untreated infection was the most likely cause, considering the extent of his injuries.

Any more playing detective would have to wait for another time. Her next appointment would be arriving soon and then three or four more after that. All her musings on the past needed to be set aside along with any speculations about the explosion at the theater or suspicions of Cyril Dankworth or questions about Kezia's Charles Dickens apparition.

An image of a pile of rocks suddenly came to mind. If Harriet could pull out one of those rocks—find the answer to just one of those mysteries—would all the other rocks come tumbling down and reveal the answers to the others?

If only she knew which rock to move.

Executive Log Entry
October 11, 1985

Every man has a price. Those who can't be bought with dollars can be bought in other, messier ways. The Gazette's owner is no exception. No more articles will appear in that gossip rag about SH until he dies.

Executive Log Entry
January 23, 2001

The Gazette *thought itself so valuable an enterprise that good money was spent putting all their news and gossip onto this world wide web. But what can be put there can also be taken away. I spent good money to make sure any reference to SH won't be found by a Nosy Nelly sitting in front of a computer.*

CHAPTER FIFTEEN

Throughout the afternoon, the sky had steadily darkened as thick, rain-filled clouds scuttled from one horizon to the other. Polly's earlier prediction of a brewing storm was coming true. A sudden clap of thunder echoed overhead. Even though Harriet was on the phone with Mitch, she hurried to the clinic's front door as the first large raindrops fell, pelting the glass like miniature waves on a rocky shore. The thunderous downpour promised to be the kind of storm she and Polly had hoped for—wild and raging outside while they were snug and dry inside.

"It's a good thing you'd already decided to spend the night in York," Harriet said to Mitch. "You're missing out on our torrential weather."

"I can't say I'm sorry about that," Mitch replied with a chuckle. "Hopefully, it'll be clear skies tomorrow and I can bring Beau home."

"I hope you can too. Don't hesitate to call if you need anything. And let me know if you find out anything new. You and Beau are in our prayers."

"Will do. Tell your husband I said hi and thanks again for the wee-hours-of-the-morning coffee."

When the call ended, Harriet returned to Polly's desk. "They've run a few tests on Beau, but nothing seems to have changed, neurologically speaking, since last time. That's good news."

Lightning streaked across the sky, near enough to momentarily brighten the vehicles parked beyond the window. Thunder quickly followed, loud and sharp. For those few moments, both Harriet and Polly froze then giggled nervously as the thunder faded.

"Your last appointment canceled because of the weather," Polly said. "I got the call when you were talking to Mitch."

"In that case, I declare the Cobble Hill Vet Clinic closed for the day." Harriet flipped the open sign to closed and locked the clinic door. "If you'd like to stay, we can have that dream evening we talked about earlier. I have a container of stew in the freezer I can heat up. I'll ask Will to pick up one of those round loaves of bread we like so much, and you can call Van and tell him to join us."

"That sounds wonderful, except for one thing."

"What's that?"

"If we're here," Polly said, "you'll feel obligated to entertain us. And you want to read your new mystery."

Harriet held up her hand. "I'd much rather enjoy a stormy night with good company. Why don't you stay?"

"You're sure Will won't mind?"

"Of course not."

"Okay then." Polly reached for her phone. "I'll see what Van is up to. If he's free, then it's a yes."

"I'll go defrost the stew. Come into the kitchen when you're done here." As Harriet left Polly to talk to her husband, Maxwell trotted-and-rolled after her. She texted Will to tell him about their potential plans then pulled the container of frozen stew from the freezer. As she was defrosting it in the microwave—though only enough to soften the edges—Polly came in from the clinic.

"We're a go," she announced. "Van is bringing the old police reports about the Hornsby accident. He didn't see anything out of the ordinary but thought you'd want to see them for yourself."

"I most certainly would." The reports might prove even more interesting to read than her novel.

Polly filled the kettle with water. "What do you hope to find in the reports?"

"The reason why Silas Hornsby fell. I mean, who smashes through an upper-level balcony railing like that?" Harriet transferred the melting stew from the container into a heavy stock pot. "Plus, it seems so odd to me that the accident happened at the theater only a couple of weeks before Eugenie's disappearance. What if the two incidents are related in some way?"

"How could they be? Unless Silas was trying to jump over the balcony and land on the stage in a vain attempt to impress Eugenie." Polly laughed at the ridiculousness of the scene she'd described. "Only to have his heart broken because she already had a boyfriend."

"You're probably right. Coincidences do happen sometimes."

"Maybe Kezia's ghost scared him so badly he fell against the railing," Polly teased as she set out cups and saucers along with a caddy of various tea bags.

"According to that newspaper article, the police made it clear the 1980s 'Top Hat Ghost' had nothing to do with the accident," Harriet said in mock seriousness. "Besides, I doubt whoever is pretending to be Kezia's ghost was around back then."

"But he might have been." Earlier that day, Polly had told Harriet that she and Kezia talked about the ghost on Saturday. Kezia described him to Polly exactly as she'd described him to Harriet—an ethereal Charles Dickens character wearing a top hat.

"Let's say whoever pretended to be the Top Hat Ghost was in his early twenties at the time. He'd be in his early sixties now," Harriet mused. "So it could be the same person. It doesn't seem very likely though. Surely the person would have grown out of such pranks."

"Maybe he found another theater to haunt. Though I've never heard any tales of the movie theater in Whitby being haunted." Polly perched on one of the island stools, and her mouth curved into a sheepish smile. "It's wrong of me to make light of what happened to Silas. Even if he didn't have any family, the county's most eligible bachelor must have had friends and admirers. And that fall had to be painful. A broken leg and a broken arm?"

Polly startled as Ash landed in her lap seemingly out of nowhere. He purred as he snuggled in her arms.

"It's hard to imagine how it happened." Harriet added additional broth to the stew then covered the stock pot with a lid. She tried to envision a scenario that made sense. One would assume Silas was sitting in a chair during the performance. Was he leaning on the balcony? Showing off in some way?

"I wish I could see the box." Harriet retrieved four soup crocks from the cupboard. "Just to get an idea what it looked like back then."

"We should see it," Polly readily agreed. "We'll ask Van to talk to Joel. Who knows? If Top Hat Ghost *did* have something to do with the accident"—Polly's eyes sparkled with mischief—"we might even find a clue to his identity."

"Wouldn't that be great?"

From beneath the island, Maxwell interrupted her scattered thoughts with a cheerful bark. He scurried to the French doors that opened onto the covered patio a fraction of a second before Will and Van appeared on the other side. They both smiled and waved.

Polly, who was closest to the doors, placed Ash on the stool and opened one of them.

"We're soaking wet." Will handed Polly the grocery bag he carried. "This sure is a rambunctious storm."

"I'll get towels." Harriet hurried into the nearby laundry room where they kept a stack of clean towels to wipe dirty paws and wrap up wet furballs who'd been out in the rain or snow. The men left their shoes outside the door and gratefully accepted the towels Harriet offered them.

Polly placed the grocery bag on the island along with the packet of papers that Van had tucked inside his jacket. Harriet eyed the packet with the eagerness of a child eyeing a plastic pumpkin full of candy. But now was not the time to dig into them. The reports weren't going anywhere, she reminded herself. There would be plenty of time after supper to read through them.

By the time the stew was bubbling hot, Will and Van were much drier and had started a fire in the living room fireplace. Harriet had decided the storm-inspired meal should be enjoyed in a place where they could lounge before the fire in the comfy chairs and sofa. She set a tray with the warmed bread, locally churned butter, and an assortment of homemade jams on the coffee table while Polly brought in another tray with water glasses and tea.

After Will said grace, they filled their bowls with the hearty stew straight from the stockpot where it was left to simmer on the kitchen stove in case anyone wanted seconds, then settled in the living room. As they ate, Harriet and Polly told their husbands about Silas Hornsby's obituary and their wish to see his box in the theater's mezzanine level.

Eventually, their conversation turned to other topics. Will asked for an update on Beau then talked about the ongoing preparations for the White Church Autumn Bazaar. Polly related funny stories about her brothers' recent antics that had them in stitches and led to the others telling their own family stories.

They'd finished their meal and were tidying the kitchen when Will's phone rang. "It's Joel," he said as he connected the call then wandered toward the study for privacy. A moment later, he returned to the kitchen, his features drawn together in a grave expression.

"Joel's been injured," he said, reaching for his jacket. "I don't know how, but he's at the theater."

"I'm coming with you." Van snatched his key from the counter. "We'll take the cruiser so we can get there faster. Should I call an ambulance?"

"He said not to."

Harriet and Polly stared at each other then turned to their husbands. "We're coming too," they said at the same time.

"In this weather?" Will stopped in the middle of putting his jacket on.

"I know he asked for you," Harriet replied. "But my training could be needed if he's badly hurt."

"That's true," Will agreed. "I'll get your bag."

Harriet slipped into her raincoat. Her veterinary bag was stocked with first-aid supplies and the equipment needed to take a person's vital signs. More than once in her career she'd been thankful for Grandad's advice to be prepared for all medical emergencies whether they involved, in words he delivered as if he were a Shakespearean actor, "man or beast."

Within a few minutes, both couples were in the cruiser, speeding toward the playhouse. As she sat in the back seat beside Polly, Harriet pondered all the misfortunes that had befallen Joel in the past few weeks.

She didn't believe in haunted theaters or Victorian ghosts or curses. But if a place could be cursed, surely that place was the Beacon.

CHAPTER SIXTEEN

Harriet peered out the cruiser's back seat window at the darkened theater. The rain still fell in a torrential downpour that significantly lessened visibility. The occasional flash of lightning, followed almost immediately by a resounding crack of thunder, lit the sky.

"Joel said all the doors are locked," Will said. "But the alarm's off, so we can open any of them without alerting the security company."

"I've got tools to get us inside." Van maneuvered his vehicle as close as he could to the steps near the back entrance and shifted the gear to park. "Did Joel say what he's doing here on a night like this?"

"He's been here most of the day," Will replied. "My guess is that he never went home."

After a brief discussion, the group decided Van would pry open the door then motion for the others to join him.

Van braced himself against the storm's onslaught then opened the driver's door. A gust of wind blew rain into the cruiser before he had climbed out and could get the door shut again. Harriet blinked against the raindrops that splattered her face. She heard the click of the cruiser's trunk as Van opened it. A moment or two later he slammed it shut and jogged to the back door.

"At least the walkway is covered," Harriet said, "though I don't suppose that roof provides much protection from this wind."

"He's going to be soaked through again, and this time there's no fireplace nearby." Worry had overcome Polly's earlier excitement, and her fearful tone caught at Harriet's heart. Van's strength had been zapped when he suffered from severe smoke inhalation from that fire a few months ago. Though he'd made a remarkable recovery, it was possible his constitution wasn't what it used to be.

Harriet clasped Polly's hand. "We'll make sure he gets warmed up inside and out," she said as optimistically as she could. "And we'll cover him in prayer just like we did before."

Polly squeezed Harriet's hand. "Thank you," she murmured.

"He did it." Will shifted in the front seat to face them with an encouraging smile. "The sidewalk and those steps may be slippery, so be careful. We don't need any sprained ankles or bruised elbows. Especially since Jinny is out of the country and isn't available to patch us up."

"I wish she were here to take care of Joel." Harriet waved her hand. "I don't mean here in this car, but at her house. Even if he doesn't want to go to the hospital, we might have persuaded him to see her."

Harriet's aunt, her dad's younger sister, had inherited the dower cottage from her father. A respected medical doctor with a deep and abiding faith, she'd lived there most of her adult life, raising her children, operating her practice from a clinic attached to the cottage, and participating in multiple church and civic activities.

Much to Harriet's delight, the dower cottage, a charming house with steep roofs and multiple chimneys, stood within a stone's throw of her own home. She'd always felt close to her aunt, even when they were separated by an ocean. But that closeness developed into a deep friendship after Harriet moved to Yorkshire. Aunt Jinny had helped her become part of her new community in ways big and small. She was a confidant, a counselor, and a much-loved kindred spirit.

"You'll have to be his doctor," Polly said.

Harriet had already accepted that fact. It wouldn't be the first time she'd checked a human's blood pressure and pulse, listened to a person's heart, or treated a wound.

The latch on Will's door clicked as he readied to push it open. He gripped Harriet's veterinary bag in his other hand. "Let's go, ladies."

Harriet closed her eyes, prayed none of them would slip or fall, and dashed to the theater's back door. Soon they were all inside the wardrobe room with the jimmied door closed behind them. Van held a huge flashlight with a wide beam, which he played around the room. The racks of clothes and dressed mannequins appeared eerie in the light and even more haunting when reflected in the wall of mirrors. He found the switch for the overhead lights, but they didn't come on when he flipped it.

"Must be the storm," he said. "Power's out."

History repeating itself. A chill raced along Harriet's spine at the unexpected thought.

"Joel is on the stairs leading to the mezzanine level." Will, holding a similar flashlight that Van had given him, led the way out of the wardrobe room.

"The theater boxes are on the mezzanine level," Harriet said. "That area is off limits. I mean, it's his theater, and he can go wherever he wants. It's strange, though, that Polly and I talked about exploring it earlier today, and now Joel is on the stairs. I'm curious why."

"You can ask him while you're treating his injuries," Will said as they crossed the left wing of the stage. With Van bringing up the rear, they hurried through the auditorium and into the lobby area.

Two sets of enclosed stairs, one on either side of the lobby, led to the mezzanine level. Usually the doors were double-padlocked, but the door nearest them stood wide open.

"Joel," Will called out as he neared the door, "it's us. Where are you?"

"Here." The feeble syllable, coming from the stairs, was followed by a groan.

Will, with Harriet close behind him, shone his beam through the open door. Joel was sprawled across the steps, face down. He twisted his head toward them, blinked, and shaded his eyes.

"Whatever happened to you?" Will asked, his tone incredulous. Harriet tried puzzling out Joel's position in the dim lighting of the flashlight, but something didn't seem right. Then she realized she couldn't see the lower part of his left leg though his knee appeared to rest on the landing.

"Please," he pleaded. "Get me out of here."

"Wait a second," Harriet cautioned. She moved in front of Will and knelt to Joel's eye level. Bruising on his temple and cheek had turned purple, and a jagged cut stretched from his eyebrow past his cheekbone. "Did you break anything?"

"I don't think so." He took a painful breath. "My leg is stuck, and I can't..." He didn't seem to have the energy to say any more.

She glanced at his knee, willing her brain to make Joel's leg make sense, then stood and shone her phone's flashlight onto the landing. From this vantage point, she could see the cracks in the wood surrounding his knee. His lower limb had gone through the landing.

"After I examine him, you and Van need to get him upright," she said to Will. "I'll be quick, but I'm worried about a concussion."

Joel groaned, and his eyes closed. For a split second, Harriet feared he'd passed out.

"Stay with me, Joel," she said in her no-nonsense voice.

"So tired," he murmured.

Polly traded places with Will in the narrow space and opened Harriet's bag. She wrapped the blood pressure cuff around Joel's upper arm, and Harriet used her stethoscope to listen to his heart and lungs. She took his pulse then his blood pressure.

"How is he?" Will asked.

"Not great." She delicately touched Joel's bruised temple. "I don't think I can do anything else until he's out of there."

As she and Polly moved to make room for Will and Van, Harriet touched Will's arm. "I know he said no ambulance, but I'm calling 999," she whispered. The number was the British equivalent to 911.

"I agree," Will said. "He should be hospitalized."

Polly dug her phone out of a deep inner pocket. "I'll do it, Harriet. You need to keep an eye on Joel while they're moving him." She stepped away to make the call.

Harriet winced along with Joel as Will and Van, as carefully and gently as they could, repositioned his free leg and got him upright. By the time Polly returned, indicating with a nod that medical services were on the way, Joel sat leaning against the stair wall with his free leg stretched along the steps. His other leg remained stuck within the wooden cracks. All four of them took off their raincoats, turned them inside out, and folded them to provide a cushion for his head, shoulders, and back as he rested.

With meaningful looks at each other, they silently agreed not to pester Joel with questions. Harriet cleaned his facial wound while Van unlocked the doors to the main entrance with the key he found in Joel's office and kept a lookout for the ambulance.

Though Joel seemed on the verge of passing out several times, he managed to stay conscious. But getting his leg caught and falling head-first down the steps had taken its toll. He'd obviously struck his head on the wall or a stairstep as he'd fallen. The jagged cut may have come from a stray nail that hadn't been hammered all the way into the wood.

The ambulance from the Whitby Medical Centre arrived faster than Harriet had expected, given the horrific weather. Will, Van, and the two emergency medical technicians worked together to pull Joel from the hole. Once he was free, they maneuvered him down the narrow steps and onto a gurney. To his credit, Joel didn't complain about going to the hospital.

Polly gave the younger EMT the vital signs that Harriet had dictated to her during her examination. Will stayed close to Joel's side while the older EMT took a new set of vitals and hooked him to an IV.

"You're going to be okay now," Will said. "These men will take good care of you."

"Come with me," Joel stammered. He licked his lips. "Don't want…to be…alone."

"I'll meet you at the hospital," Will promised. "As soon as I can get there."

Joel nodded, his eyes still closed. Harriet wrapped her arm around Will's, giving him quiet encouragement and support.

"A body's got to be careful in old places like this," the older EMT said. "One wrong step, and look what happened to this fella. Completely stuck until someone comes along to get him out. Those stairs need to be repaired before anyone else gets hurt."

Joel's facial muscles twisted into a strange grimace. "Already done."

Will exchanged a glance with Harriet then turned back to Joel. "What do you mean? What's 'already done'?"

Joel took a deep breath then opened his eyes. "Stairs. Already done."

"The landing wasn't," Will said. "Or this wouldn't have happened."

"Done," Joel insisted. "Piers."

Will couldn't hide his confusion. "Pierce?"

"Not 'pierce,'" Harriet said. "Piers."

Joel nodded.

"Piers Berrycloth?" Will asked. "The contractor?"

"Fixed."

"But—"

Harriet interrupted Will by squeezing his arm. This wasn't the time or place to argue with Joel about what the contractor had or hadn't done.

"I'll talk to Piers in the morning," Will said, making sure to keep his tone upbeat for Joel's sake. "Have him come and look at the stairs."

"That's a great idea." Harriet smiled at Joel even though his eyes were closed.

"We're ready to go now," the younger EMT said, placing a hand on Joel's shoulder. "My partner is backing up the ambulance as close to the entrance as he can, but I can't guarantee you won't get wet unless I put a plastic tarp over you. Are you okay with that?"

Joel slowly nodded, then his fingers twitched. He stretched out his hand, and Will took it in his. "You're okay, buddy. You'll be at the medical center soon, and they'll take good care of you. The staff is one of the best in the country."

"Pocket," Joel rasped as he smacked his other palm against his side. "Pocket."

"Do you have something in your pocket?" Harriet asked. "Something for Will?"

Joel's head moved a fraction of an inch. Judging from his reaction, it must have burst into incredible pain. Harriet bent toward him. "Breathe," she said. "Breathe with me."

She took long, deep breaths and was gratified when Joel measured his breaths against hers. "That's good," she said. "You're doing fine."

"Pocket." His fingers twitched again.

Will shrugged then checked Joel's pocket. He pulled out a folded scrap of paper and opened it. As he read the handwritten words, his eyes widened in shock.

"What does it say?" Harriet asked with concern.

He handed it to her so she could read it for herself.

Silas Hornsby was murdered.

CHAPTER SEVENTEEN

*P**lease don't let it be true!* Harriet's stunned reaction when she read the handwritten words, a heartfelt plea, still resonated with her, even though more than twelve hours had passed since Will handed her the note. The EMTs had whisked Joel away—as they needed to do—before she or Will could ask him any details about the scrap of paper he'd had in his pocket.

And Harriet had so many questions. Who had written the cryptic note? Where had he gotten it? Why would anyone bring up the forty-year-old "accident" now? Did the accusation have something to do with the theater reopening, or was it a confession?

More than anything else, Harriet wanted to know—needed to know—if Silas Hornsby's death, whether an accident or murder, was somehow related to Eugenie Okehurst's disappearance.

At least now she could surmise why Joel had gone to the mezzanine level. No doubt he'd wanted to look around the box with the broken railing after reading the strange message.

Because of the other notes Joel had received, Will had immediately turned this one over to Van, who slid it into an evidence bag. If any fingerprints were found on it, she and Will would have to be printed. Joel too. That way, any prints other than theirs would be considered suspect.

"I told him to be careful if he received any more notes," Will had moaned after finally telling Van about the previous threatening notes. "Not to handle them and definitely not to shove them into his pocket." But in Joel's defense, this note hadn't been like the others. Those had been typed on a computer and printed onto copier paper. This one was written in block letters with blue ink on a scrap of stationery that had obviously been torn from a larger sheet. And this note wasn't threatening in any way. So did someone else write this one?

After the ambulance took Joel away, Van dropped Harriet and Will off at Cobble Hill Farm. Will kept his promise to Joel and immediately drove to the Whitby Medical Centre. Harriet thought about going with him but decided Joel needed rest more than she needed answers. Besides, her lack of sleep was catching up with her.

She kissed Will goodbye then tended to their pets and tidied the living room and kitchen. Once the chores were finished, she settled in the reading nook with the packet Van had brought her. Between stifling yawns, she scanned the investigative reports.

Unfortunately, she found nothing definitive in the sparse notes. Similar to the results of the Okehurst investigation, Harriet felt that Silas Hornsby's alleged accident wasn't aggressively investigated by the 1980s law enforcement officials who seemed to accept the easiest solution without question. Foul play was practically unthinkable. The railing broke, and Silas Hornsby fell. Case closed.

If the same incident occurred today, Harriet had no doubt that Van would dot every *i* and cross every *t* before coming to a conclusion.

All these thoughts whirled around in Harriet's mind as she and Will arrived at the theater on Tuesday morning to meet Piers

Berrycloth, the contractor in charge of supervising the renovations. He'd seemed truly shocked to learn of Joel's injury and was waiting for them at the lobby entrance.

After a round of subdued greetings, Will unlocked the doors with the key that Van had given him the night before. Fortunately, the power had been restored sometime during the wee morning hours, and the trio headed for the mezzanine stairway. The door to the enclosed stairs stood wide open, as they'd left it last night.

"Tell me again what happened," Piers said to Will. He was below average in height and had the wiry build of a bronco rider Harriet had seen at a rodeo her family attended when they were on vacation in Wyoming. Beneath the contractor's quiet demeanor was a wealth of expertise gained by years of tackling electrical, plumbing, and carpentry projects on many of the historic homes in the area.

"From what I understand," Will said, "Joel had gone to the mezzanine level. On his way back down, his foot went through the landing, and he fell forward. His leg was stuck up to his knee, and his body was twisted in such a way that he couldn't get up."

"I told him repairs needed to be made to this level," Piers said. "All the details are in my original report."

"He said you'd already fixed these stairs."

Piers's already ruddy complexion turned an even deeper shade of red. "Obviously, I haven't, or Mr. Elphick wouldn't have fallen through the floor. That's why this door was kept double-locked. To keep anyone foolish enough to go up there from getting themselves hurt."

Instead of contradicting the contractor, Will shifted his stance and glanced at Harriet. He knew, as did she, that, despite his halting speech, Joel had been adamant the work on the stairs had already been completed. She understood why Will didn't want to flat out accuse Piers of lying. Neither did she. He'd worked on a few projects at Cobble Hill Farm, and she'd found his reputation of being fully competent and knowledgeable, reliable, and reasonably priced to be spot-on.

"There must be a misunderstanding," she said. "DC Worthington already took photographs of the—"

Piers's eyes rounded. "Why would he do that?"

"In case it wasn't an accident," Harriet answered him, keeping her voice as calm as the North Sea on a windless day. Even though Will had explained that Joel didn't want an investigation, Van wasn't happy to have been left in the dark about the notes or about Cyril Dankworth's blustering in the diner. Once he knew Joel had been threatened, he insisted on treating the incident as suspicious until proven otherwise.

"There was no misunderstanding," Piers insisted. "I won't stand here and be falsely accused, not even by you, Pastor."

Will held up his hands as if in surrender. "I'm not accusing you of anything."

"Then why am I here?"

"As Harriet was about to say before she was interrupted, we want to help Joel out as much as possible while he's convalescing." Will's expression softened as he smiled at Piers. "We hoped you could provide an estimate for making the repairs, both in time and money. I can't say if or when Joel will want the work done, but at least he'll have the information he needs."

Seemingly mollified, Piers relaxed his facial features and shoulders. "Obviously, the broken boards need to be replaced. I can put a piece of plywood over the landing until Mr. Elphick makes a decision. That way he won't fall through should he get a notion to go up there again."

"I'm sure he'd appreciate that." Will extended his hand, and Piers clasped it. "I know I do."

"I'll get right on that, Pastor."

While Will and Piers inspected the stairs and the landing, Harriet made her way to the back corridor. Once they knew no one had been injured in Saturday's explosion, she'd told Will she'd been disappointed that the scare ruined her plans to see the antique items that Kezia and Andrew had collected for the play.

As long as the door to the workroom was unlocked, this was Harriet's chance to have her own private viewing of the antiques and collectibles. She walked past the wardrobe room but halted at the dressing room door that had been assigned to her, Polly, Elena, and Ada. No one she'd gone to college or veterinary school with would have ever believed her name would be displayed so prominently.

It didn't matter that she shared the honor with three of her friends or that everyone in the production was an amateur. It was still an honor to be celebrated.

She slipped her phone from her bag and took a picture to send to her parents. They'd laugh to see proof that she was now a star. After taking a couple of photos of the sign and a few more selfies of her standing beside the sign, she tried the handle. The door easily swung open, and Harriet switched her camera to the video setting. For the next minute or so, she filmed a tour of the dressing room to send to her family. Given the time difference between Yorkshire and Connecticut, she needed to wait to send text messages with the photos and video until later that afternoon.

The name card stuck into the mirror frame on her antique vanity was slightly askew. Harriet straightened it then lowered herself to the padded, metal-backed chair. An amateur production this might be, but even after all the hours of rehearsal she'd gone though, Harriet could hardly believe this star treatment was happening to her. The whole thing came with a surreal quality that tempted her to pinch her arm to see if she was dreaming.

Instead of giving in to that painful temptation, she propped her chin in her hand and studied her reflection as she practiced a smattering of expressions.

Elizabeth overhearing Darcy's "she's tolerable enough, I suppose." Elizabeth's humiliating shock at hearing Mr. Collins's proposal followed by her self-righteous anger at hearing Darcy's. Elizabeth discovering the herculean efforts Darcy had undertaken to save her family from scandal.

The exercise amused her and scared her at the same time. She hoped and prayed she did justice to the much-admired character for all the *Pride and Prejudice* fans who'd be sitting in the audience when she performed the iconic role.

As she had the day Polly showed her the room, Harriet once more checked out the contents of the vanity drawers. Strange. The makeup kits and brushes didn't appear to be as neatly arranged as they had been the other day. Perhaps the simple act of opening and closing the drawer had caused the items to shift, though that seemed unlikely.

"Maybe Kezia's Dickensian ghost needed to powder his nose," she said to her reflection. She made a mental note to once again ask Will about talking to the Corbin brothers. There was so much going on with the church bazaar and the theater, the poor guy had little time to talk to Harriet let alone have a serious conversation with Joshua and Caleb. She didn't want to push him into anything, but a little nudge would most likely turn out to be a good thing.

She checked out the two bottom drawers that had been empty on Saturday. Both were still empty, but one was partially open. She attempted to close it, but though it had worked perfectly a few days ago, now it refused to shut.

Frustrated with the unwieldy drawer, Harriet pulled it all the way out of the vanity and peered into the interior space. No wonder it wouldn't close properly. A padded envelope had somehow fallen behind the drawer and been pushed to the back.

Harriet tugged the thick envelope from its hiding space and stared at the words handwritten across the front.

To Miss Elizabeth Bennet

Private & Personal

"I guess that's me," Harriet said to her reflection. She took a deep breath and opened the flap. Inside she found a woman's wallet made of imitation textured leather.

"How in the world...," she muttered, hesitating only a moment before opening it. Several photo sleeves were on one side and a change pocket was on the other. The first photo sleeve held a driver's license issued to Eugenie Amelia Okehurst.

Harriet could hardly believe her eyes. How was it possible she was holding Eugenie's wallet?

The driver's license photo, unlike the printout of the black-and-white publicity photo in the Beacon/Okehurst folder, captured Eugenie's classic girl-next-door innocence. Her blue eyes stared at the camera as if she had a secret she wanted to share with the world.

The remaining sleeves held two snapshots. There were no coins in the change pocket nor was there any money in the bills compartment.

Multiple questions raced through Harriet's mind. Had Eugenie been so excited about her upcoming elopement that she forgot her wallet? Wouldn't she have needed her photo identification when she got to Gretna Green? Shouldn't there have been at least a dollar or two in the bills slot? Or a few random coins in the change pocket? Had Eugenie often traveled without any money? Or had she taken all her money and somehow managed to forget her wallet?

It was possible, Harriet supposed, that Eugenie had left her wallet behind on purpose. Maybe it was meant to be a kind of clue, perhaps to convince the person she expected to find it that the elopement story was a sham. Had she hoped that individual would contact law enforcement and raise an alarm?

If that had been her plan, it failed miserably.

Or what if this vanity had once belonged to Eugenie Okehurst, and she was the *Miss Elizabeth Bennet* meant to find the envelope?

Impossible. The envelope looked too new to have been in that cavity for the past forty years.

Even so, Harriet couldn't ignore a potential lead, no matter how impossible it appeared. She released a heavy sigh as she prepared to make a phone call then searched for the number to the Ellsworths' store in her phone's contacts list. When the call rang, she prayed Kezia would answer and have a few moments to talk. Her prayers were answered on the third ring.

"It's me, Harriet," she said. "I know this may sound strange, but your grandmother told me that you refinished some of the furniture pieces here at the theater. Did that include the dressing table vanities?"

"I refinished the ones we put into the star dressing room," Kezia replied. "You were assigned one of those. Why do you ask? Is something wrong with one of them?"

Harriet took a deep breath before answering. She couldn't very well avoid Kezia's questions when she was the one who'd started the conversation. "I found an envelope behind one of the drawers. Is it possible you overlooked it?"

"No way. What kind of envelope was it?"

"A typical nine-by-twelve white padded envelope," Harriet replied. "It had a wallet inside. The driver's license has Eugenie Okehurst's name and photograph on it."

"Isn't she the actress who played Elizabeth Bennet forty years ago?"

"The very same."

"I don't know what to tell you," Kezia said. "I disassembled every one of the vanities in that room, sanded them, stained them, and put them together again. If there'd been an envelope either in or behind one of the drawers, especially one big enough to hold a wallet, I would have seen it."

"That's what I thought. I just wanted to find out for sure." Harriet stared at the open wallet lying on top of the vanity. Eugenie's blue eyes seemed to stare back at her.

Kezia's voice coming through the phone's speaker interrupted Harriet's thoughts. "Someone played a trick on me with that silly ghost, and now someone is playing a trick on you."

"By hiding Eugenie's wallet in my vanity? Giving me her driver's license? What kind of trick is that?"

"The license is probably a fake. The best thing to do is absolutely nothing. Don't give this prankster the satisfaction of seeing you react in any way. That's my advice."

Kezia Ellsworth, your name is Charlotte Lucas.

Seriously, Joel's casting for the extremely practical and sensible Charlotte, Elizabeth's close friend who marries for security instead of love, was spot-on. Though surely not when it came to Kezia's marriage to Andrew, Harriet chided herself. The two were much more suited to each other than Charlotte and Mr. Collins. But when it came to Charlotte's general outlook on life, Kezia was the perfect choice to play her.

"I'm not sure I can pretend I didn't find it."

"That's because you have too much of Elizabeth Bennet in you." Kezia chuckled. "Sorry, Harriet, but I need to go. I'm in the store by myself and a tourist quartet just walked in."

When the call ended, Harriet slid the drawer back in place. This time it shut flush with the desk. She once again stared at her reflection as she held up the wallet. "If this belongs to Eugenie, then I think someone is trying to tell me that she didn't go to Gretna Green. She didn't write the letter to Layla Hastings. And it seems she never acted again."

Harriet shifted her gaze from her reflection to the photograph of the young woman—in many ways only a girl.

"What in the world happened to you?"

CHAPTER EIGHTEEN

Harriet, on her way to find Will, was entering the lobby when Odette swept toward her. She wore a loose caftan over flowing pants and a turtleneck, all in various shades of gray and black. A russet and gold scarf was stylishly knotted at her neck, her salt-and-pepper coiled hair done in a neat but elaborate updo. While she maintained her regal bearing, the fine lines around her mouth and eyes seemed more pronounced, and her breathing sounded slightly irregular.

"Is it true what I've heard about Mr. Elphick?" she asked, not bothering to offer a conventional greeting.

Harriet's natural impulse was to say, "that depends on what you've heard," but she doubted Odette would appreciate such a frivolous attempt at humor.

"He fell last night when he was here alone." Harriet went on to tell her what had happened, without mentioning the scrap of paper he'd had in his pocket. Odette stood still as a statue during Harriet's explanation. Not a single emotion flickered across her stony face.

When Harriet finished telling as much as she felt she could, Odette averted her gaze and pressed her hand against her stomach. "He will be fine, no?"

"His ankle is sprained, and he needs time to heal from his cuts and bruises," Harriet replied. She offered a comforting smile. "Will talked to him a few minutes this morning. He has a mild concussion, and he's eager to escape. As soon as he's released, Will plans to pick him up."

"It's a relief to know his injuries weren't worse and that he has such a good friend looking after him. Is foul play suspected?"

"That's a strange question to ask. Why would you think so?"

"One hears rumors." Odette lifted a shoulder in a nonchalant shrug. "Sees strange things."

"Such as?"

Odette pulled in her bottom lip, an unusually vulnerable gesture for someone who always seemed in total control of her movements, as a long moment passed between the two women.

"A top hat on nobody's head," she murmured. "A Victorian coat where it does not belong."

"The clothes of a ghost." Harriet purposely made the words into a statement instead of a question that Odette might refuse to answer.

"Do you believe in such things?"

"Not in ghosts, nor haunted buildings."

"And yet…" Odette struck a pose. "'There are more things in heaven and earth, Horatio'—or should I say Harriet—'than are dreamt of in your philosophy.'"

"Said Hamlet to his friend after he talked to his father's spirit."

Odette's emotionless facade eased as an amused smile softened her expression. "You know your Shakespeare."

"Only the famous quotes. Where are the top hat and Victorian coat now?"

"Come with me, and I'll show you."

Curiouser and curiouser. The literary neuron in Harriet's brain leaped from Shakespeare's *Hamlet* to Lewis Carroll's *Alice in Wonderland.* She glanced at Will, who hadn't yet noticed her. He seemed to be taking Piers to the electrical room where the explosion had occurred, so Harriet followed after Odette.

The older woman led the way to the alcove where the access to the stage-left crossover was located. The crossover in this theater was a series of wooden catwalks located above the stage and out of sight of the audience.

Odette pointed to a scuffed black trunk with broken leather straps and multiple travel stickers. It sat in a corner along with cracked crates and cobweb-covered shelving. "Open it and see for yourself."

Harriet was unsure if she should be nosing around in the alcove. Especially one with spiders. But her curiosity overcame her hesitation, and she approached the trunk. Unlike the crates and shelves and most of the trunk, the metallic clasps were free of dust. Harriet unlatched them and lifted the lid.

A black top hat and rumpled coat lay on top of a pile of faded and torn clothing. Harriet wrinkled her nose at the musty odor that wafted from the raggedy fabrics.

"How did you find this?" she asked.

Odette slowly lifted her shoulder. "I have worked in several theaters that boast of a ghost. Often these stories bring in tourists who trade their pounds and shillings for the thrill of the unknown. Perhaps those stories are true, perhaps they are not. It's not for me to say."

She bent beside the trunk and lifted out the hat. "The mysteries of the Beacon-on-the-Moor didn't occur in the days of Dickens.

Why would its ghost be from that era? I explore. I look where others do not. I find what is hidden."

Harriet understood that Odette's question was rhetorical, so she responded with a question of her own. "What mysteries?" she asked.

"The same mysteries that capture your imagination." Odette's smile was as enigmatic as the Mona Lisa's as she twirled the hat between her bejeweled fingers. "The dying bachelor. The disappearing actress."

"I am intrigued by their stories," Harriet readily admitted. "What do you know about them?"

"I hear the rumors told by idle gossips, and I listen to the reminisces shared by those old enough to remember the events." She tossed the top hat into the trunk and waved her hand over the coat. "Take a closer look and tell me what you see."

Harriet squatted beside Odette, careful to place her hand on a dust-free spot of the trunk to support herself as she peered at the coat. She frowned in disbelief at the blue flecks scattered on the coat's collar and shoulder. "Are those pastry crumbs?"

"I believe so, though I haven't tasted one to be sure." Odette wrinkled her nose.

Harriet studied the crumbs. "Poppy Schofield decorates a blueberry pastry braid with an icing that same shade of blue," she said. "I ate one once and had crumbs all along the front of my sweater."

"Ah, yes. Poppy often brings us goodies from her shop. I've enjoyed that blueberry pastry braid too. It appears to be a favorite of our stage crew."

"Joshua and Caleb?"

Odette held Harriet's gaze, as if willing her to follow the trail she'd placed before her.

"I've wondered if they were responsible for all this haunting nonsense."

"Boys will be boys, I suppose, and there's been no real harm. After the initial shocks and chills, the cast seems amused by the idea that the theater is haunted."

"Joel mentioned something like that too." Harriet studied the crumb-flecked coat again. Something nagged at her...but what was it? "Will has been meaning to talk to them about putting childish things behind them, but he hasn't had the chance."

"Maybe it's enough for us to know they're the culprits, and let them have their fun."

Harriet wasn't sure she agreed but wasn't in the mood to argue the point. "I'd like to know how they did it."

"The ghost?" Odette shrugged then lowered the trunk's lid. "Easily done with the right equipment and software."

She clasped the latches then rose. "I must be off. No matter how many alterations I make, there always seems to be at least one more."

Harriet watched her go then opened the trunk again. She gingerly fingered one of the crumbs then dusted a few from the collar. They easily fell away from the cloth.

The proverbial light bulb went off, illuminating the reason behind the nagging itch.

The trunk had provided a backdrop where the coat was a character. The crumbs were props someone had scattered on the fabric *after* it had been placed in the trunk.

Everything Odette had shown Harriet was staged.

Staged by Odette? To what purpose?

Harriet grabbed her phone and took several photos of the open trunk with close-ups on the top hat and the Victorian coat. She also took photos after she closed the trunk to show how it was positioned among the crates.

As much as she wanted to pull the coat out of the trunk and examine it, she refused to give in to the impulse. She didn't want to inadvertently tamper with any evidence that might connect Kezia's Dickensian ghost to a prankster. Or, in a worst-case scenario, someone with more nefarious motives than a couple of high-spirited teenagers.

She started to go in search of Will, but when she reached the door, she paused. With all the other strange things that had happened recently, was she crazy to believe the clothes or the trunk might disappear before she returned with him? Sure, she had her photos. But she needed him to see the physical evidence. No one was going to tamper with the crumbs, the coat, or the trunk without going through her first. She might as well make herself comfortable right here.

She retrieved a folding chair and settled in the doorway leading to the stage wings. In less than a minute, the photos she'd taken were on their way to Will with a brief text.

FOUND KEZIA'S GHOST. MEET ME IN STAGE LEFT CROSSOVER ALCOVE.

Now all she had to do was wait for Will to show up.

She planted her elbows on her knees and rested her chin in her hands. Hopefully, she'd get a good night's sleep sometime soon. Maybe after the ghost had been caught, she found Eugenie, the cast of the play had their final curtain call, and the autumn bazaar was over. Until then, she'd take a catnap whenever she could and for however long she could.

Which wasn't nearly as long as she would have liked.

Will's voice grew louder as he neared the crossover. Who was he talking to? Harriet lifted her head and smiled at him and Van when they turned the corner from the lobby.

"I didn't know you were already here," she said to Van as Will extended a hand to help her to her feet. "But I'm glad you are so you can see this too."

"I wanted to hear what Piers had to say about the rotten wood in the landing," Van said. "And see the hole for myself now that the power has been restored. It was all but impossible to investigate it last night."

Even though Harriet was eager to show the trunk to the two men, she also wanted to know Van's perspective on what had happened to Joel. "What's your professional opinion?" she asked him.

"It doesn't take a professional to know the wood was rotten," Van replied. "The break is more jagged than I realized last night, and there are traces of blood on the edges. It's no wonder Joel was in so much pain."

"I talked to him about ten minutes ago," Will added. "He said the doctor had to stitch up a couple of nasty gashes on his shin and calf."

"Poor guy." Harriet couldn't imagine how awful it must have been for Joel to be caught in the broken wood the way he had been. Each minute must have felt like an hour.

Will leaned against the doorframe. "He insisted Piers had already fixed the landing. And Piers still insists he hadn't."

"Which means there was a giant breakdown in communication," Van said. "Or one of them is lying."

Harriet cringed at the suggestion that either man was deliberately being deceitful. Piers had an impeccable reputation in the community that he'd built up over decades. Joel was a newcomer to the area and, as he himself admitted, had been careless with the truth in the past. But Harriet believed he'd changed. Surely he wouldn't risk Will's friendship and goodwill by making false accusations against Piers.

"I pray it's a breakdown in communication," she said.

"Me too," Will murmured.

Harriet's heart went out to him. He'd be so hurt if Joel was lying. Though he'd be disappointed if Piers was lying too. *Please, Lord. Don't let anyone be lying.*

She caught the sympathetic glance that Van sent Will's way. He also understood how hard this entire episode could turn out to be for his friend. Van shifted his gaze to Harriet.

"Tell me more about these photos you sent Will," he said.

Harriet smiled her gratitude that he'd changed the subject. Mostly for Will's sake, but also for her own. She was beyond ready to let them in on what Odette had shown her. And to talk out her half-formed suspicions.

"Keep in mind that Kezia told both Polly and me that her ghost was wearing a top hat and looked like he'd stepped out of a Dickens novel." Harriet went on to brief them on how Odette had brought her into the alcove, then she dramatically opened the trunk to reveal the top hat and the crumb-scattered coat.

"Don't touch anything," Van warned as he took his own series of photos. Then he stepped back and stared at the trunk's contents. "Something seems off here," he finally said.

Yes! Harriet inwardly cheered. "I'm so glad you said that. I was afraid my imagination was playing tricks on me."

Will frowned as he studied the trunk. "What do you mean? I don't get it."

Van gestured to the coat. "The crumbs. They're too perfect."

"Of course." Will grinned as if relieved to be in on a secret. "It looks like someone tossed the crumbs on the coat after it was placed inside the trunk."

"Like it was staged, right?" Harriet said.

"That's what it looks like to me." Van managed to get one of the larger crumbs on the tip of his finger and studied it. "This appears to have come from one of those blueberry pastry braids from the Biscuit Bistro."

"Odette and I think the same. She said that Joshua and Caleb love those."

Van's brows drew together. "So we're to believe that one of the Corbin brothers got dressed up as a ghost and ate blueberry pastry braids as they haunted the theater? Then put the crumb-covered coat in this trunk?"

"I think someone—maybe Odette—wants us to believe that." Harriet recounted their conversation, including Odette's suggestion that they let the teens have their fun. "I get the sense that she wants to pin the blame on Joshua and Caleb but doesn't want anyone to confront them. Which doesn't make sense."

"Not to us, perhaps," Will reasoned. "I'm not sure theater folk think the same as ordinary citizens."

"'Citizens?'" Van's skeptical tone earned a chuckle from Will.

"Anyone who isn't in the theater," Will explained. "It seems to me that Odette enjoys drama. But she doesn't want this to get out of control or get the boys into real trouble. This was her way of letting you know the truth and asking you to let it go."

The more Harriet considered Will's reasoning, the more she believed he was right. She also couldn't help wondering what other kind of drama Odette might be enjoying. Did the enigmatic seamstress have more secrets up her caftan sleeve?

CHAPTER NINETEEN

Since all the rehearsals were canceled because of Joel's injury, the crew didn't need to come to the theater that day. From Harriet's perspective, that made it even stranger that Odette had shown up. Though her concern for Joel appeared genuine, did she have other reasons for being at the Beacon? Was she really protecting the Corbin brothers? Or was she framing them? Was she the one who had hidden a runaway actress's wallet in a dressing table?

Van placed the top hat and coat in evidence bags on the off chance that the appearance of the ghost and the explosion were somehow related. Then Harriet showed him and Will the wallet. "Kezia refinished the vanity," she told them. "The envelope wasn't in it then."

After Van examined the drawers, he said, "Seems to me like you were meant to find it."

"I agree," Will said. "The question is, why?"

"I've been asking myself the same question," Harriet said. "Maybe someone doesn't want me to stop searching for Eugenie. Or maybe one of these photographs is a clue, and it's up to me to figure it out."

She focused her gaze on Van. "Is the wallet evidence in her missing person's case?"

"That case was closed forty years ago," Van replied. "DI McCormick hasn't decided to reopen it, so right now it's not even considered a cold case. Why don't you give me the driver's license so I can do a check on it? You can keep the wallet, but take good care of it in case circumstances change and we need it."

"You know where to find me if you do." Harriet gave Van the license then tucked the wallet into her sling bag while Will slid the drawers back into the dressing table. With that settled, now would be a good time to switch gears and investigate the balcony.

"Since we're here," she said, adding a note of playful pleading to her tone, "could we take a look at the mezzanine boxes?"

"All the boxes, or one particular box?" The sparkle in Will's eyes made it clear he already knew the answer.

Harriet held up one finger. "Do you think it'd be okay?" she asked him.

"Not if one of us falls through the hole in the landing," he said.

"Or we could take the other set of stairs," Harriet suggested.

"That doesn't make it any safer," Will pointed out. "Plus, that door is still double-locked." He glanced at Van. "Help me out here."

Van held up his hands as if in surrender. "Nope," he said. "I'm not getting involved in a domestic."

Will laughed. "We're not having a domestic. This isn't even a spat."

"Still not getting involved."

"Aren't either of you curious?" Harriet asked. "No one has used that box since Silas Hornsby fell. The police barely investigated." Her eyes darted to Van. "No offense."

"None taken." He picked up the evidence bags he'd placed on Polly's dressing table. "I'm going to investigate the mystery that's happening now and leave the past mysteries to the two of you. Joel told me where to find a couple of those other threatening notes he received, so I need to process them too. See you two later."

Once he left, Harriet took Will's hand. "I know what you're thinking. We shouldn't go to the mezzanine level without Joel's permission. And you're absolutely right. It's just that I can't help feeling there's more to the story than what I've read in the police reports and in the newspaper. Plus, I'm almost certain that's why Joel went to the mezzanine level. He read that note and wanted to see the scene of the crime."

"Crime?"

"Possible crime?"

At that moment, Will's phone buzzed. He glanced at the screen, grinned, and held it up for Harriet to read the screen.

Joel Elphick.

"It's a sign," Harriet said with a chuckle.

Will held her gaze as he answered the call.

"Hi, Joel. Are you ready to leave the hospital?"

Since Will hadn't put the call on speaker, all Harriet could hear was the murmur of Joel's voice.

"I'll be there." More murmuring. "Before I let you go, Harriet is here. She wants to ask you something." Will pressed the speaker button while Harriet gave him a shocked "you-did-not" look. His grin grew even bigger.

She quickly composed herself, pretending to shoot eye-daggers at Will. "How are you, Joel?"

"Better than I should be," he answered. Even though he attempted a light tone, Harriet detected the pain in his voice. "Wishing I hadn't been foolish enough to poke around upstairs."

Harriet turned his words around to make them her own. "Would it be foolish for me to go up there?"

Without giving him a chance to respond, she rushed on. "Did you know Silas Hornsby fell from one of the balcony boxes? At the time, the police concluded it was an accident and closed the case. But I don't think so, and apparently whoever wrote you that note doesn't think so either." She might have continued on if she hadn't run out of breath.

For a long moment, the line was silent. Then Joel's voice came through the speaker. "It's not safe."

"I'll be extra careful."

"I've heard you're good at solving mysteries, so I won't say no. I want to know more about how this Silas guy fell too." Joel blew out a breath. "All I ask is that you don't go up there by yourself. I can't have my Elizabeth Bennet on crutches. Or worse."

"I'll go with her," Will cut in. "We've got time before we need to head to Whitby to pick you up."

The call ended after Joel told Will where to find the keys to the second stairway door. Excitement sent adrenaline through Harriet. Finally, a chance to see the scene of the fall.

Which she was all but certain was the scene of a crime.

The box was easy to find, since the missing balcony railing was evident from the point of view of anyone standing on the stage. Harriet had noticed the damaged box during rehearsals before she'd ever heard anything about Silas Hornsby or his fall.

All the curtains that had once separated the boxes from the corridor had been removed. The only reason Harriet even knew there had been curtains at one time was from Joel's collection of old photographs. Each box had eight seats divided into two rows of four with an aisle on one side. The burgundy upholstery was marred with water stains and what appeared to be chewed-up holes.

Mice? Harriet shivered.

The brocade wallpaper must have seemed opulent at one time, but now it was faded and torn. Photographs of actors and actresses who'd once performed on the Beacon stage decorated the walls, but the cracks in the glass and the dust-coated frames added to the heavy sense of decay and age.

A couple of the boxes in the center of the mezzanine appeared as if someone had made at least a half-hearted effort to clean them but quit before finishing the monumental task. No wonder Joel needed to wait for more financing to implement Phase Two of his renovation plan.

Harriet and Will, watching out for weak floorboards, entered the box where Silas Hornsby attended his last theater performance. It was similar to the other boxes they'd seen, though perhaps with even more litter on the floor.

She walked down the broad steps to the railing, heeding Will's warning not to get too close to the edge. He needn't have worried, since she had no intention of repeating Silas's fate.

Faded burgundy bunting still hung in several places from the box. Will tested the railing at one end by giving it a firm shake. At least he tried.

"It's strong here," he announced when the railing didn't budge. He moved closer to the gap and tried again with no more success. "I wonder if someone reinforced the remaining railing afterward. Though why anyone would go to such bother to reattach the torn bunting is beyond me."

He swatted at the frayed edges of the bunting then fingered the cloth as if deep in thought.

"What are you thinking?" Harriet stood close to the aisle seat in the front row. Silas had sat in one of those seats, most likely the aisle seat or the one next to it, based on the location of the gap. But that detail hadn't been recorded in the police investigation reports or in the newspaper articles she had read.

"I don't know for sure," Will replied. "This fabric supposedly ripped when the railing fell away. That seems reasonable. It's not strong enough to prevent his fall, but it might have broken it."

Harriet moved to the seat farthest from the aisle and fingered the bunting near the wall. Though the fabric was thick—and surprisingly greasy to the touch—she agreed with Will's assessment.

Will took a section of the fabric in both hands and pulled. "It's too strong for me to rip it apart." He studied the frayed edge again. "Hornsby must have fallen hard, but these edges seem too clean to have been caused by that."

He tugged the bunting away from the remaining edge of the horizontal railing and shone his phone's flashlight on the exposed wood. "Take a look at this. The break is a little jagged, but the top bit could be a clean cut. The bottom bit too."

A surge of excitement sped through Harriet quicker than a lightning bolt. "Do you think someone cut the railing?"

"It's possible. Not by making a straight cut though. It appears they cut from the top and the bottom then angled the cut in between to meet them. Clever work, but anyone studying it can see what they did."

Harriet moved closer to the railing and checked out the torn bunting while Will studied the railing on the other side of the gap. The rip in the fabric wasn't so much a rip as a cut.

"The edge of this railing looks the same as the other one," Will said. "I'm almost sure these cuts were made deliberately."

"Which means Silas's fall wasn't an accident."

"I don't know if a jury would agree, but no. I don't think so."

Harriet's momentary excitement faded as she considered the ramifications of Will's findings. If he was right, then someone had tampered with the railing and the bunting in a successful attempt to make a deliberate act appear like an accident.

But because Silas had eventually died because of his injuries, his enemy was guilty of murder.

Executive Log Entry
October 5, 1985

The investigation will soon end, and the constable will retire with a bonus.

The Beacon will close—I'll see to that. What should have been mine will fall into ruin.

CHAPTER TWENTY

While taking Joel home from the Whitby Medical Centre, Harriet and Will filled him in on everything that happened that morning. His shoulders appeared to bow beneath the weight of so much news, but he insisted on knowing as many details as possible.

"How can so many strange things be happening at the same time?" The question was obviously meant as a rhetorical one, but Harriet wished she had an answer for him.

"An actress who may or may not have eloped," Joel continued. "A prominent citizen who died after an injury that may or may not have been deliberate. An explosion that may or may not have been sabotage. And none of that includes the strange noises, cold air spots, and a ghost straight out of Dickens that apparently loves Poppy Schofield's blueberry pastry braids."

"It's a lot to process," Harriet said, wanting to encourage him as much as possible though she couldn't help but notice he didn't mention the uncertainties of his own injury. "Even more so when you consider that Eugenie's and Silas's mysteries occurred so close to the theater closing while the others are happening now that it's preparing to open it again."

"See what I mean?" Joel exclaimed. "Our opening performance is supposed to be in three days, but the show can't go on until DI

McCormick and Chief Royan release the findings from their joint investigation. Meanwhile, all this other nonsense is happening. We're missing an entire day of scene rehearsals because my foot went through a crack in the floor that was supposed to have been fixed."

He paused to blow out a breath then waved his hand in an apologetic gesture. "I didn't mean to go on a rant. But I admit, I'm scared. Someone wants the Beacon to fail and is doing everything possible to make that happen. I wish I knew why."

Harriet wished she did too, and that she could do something to lessen Joel's stress.

Half an hour later, Will dropped Harriet off at the police station. Van had called and asked her to go with him to see the Corbin brothers.

They found the teens spending their unexpected free day in the family garage, which they'd turned into an adolescent's version of a man cave. Though both boys were technically adults, Van asked Ruby to stay around while he talked to them.

"I suppose you know why I'm here," Van said.

"We didn't break any laws," Joshua said. "Just wanted to have some fun. That's all."

Van responded with his best constable glare, and the boys confessed everything. Talking over each other, they readily—and proudly—explained the technicalities of creating the haunting noises and the cold spots.

Harriet and Ruby exchanged a "what language are they speaking?" glance with each other.

The brothers also admitted to projecting the ethereal image that frightened Kezia.

"We didn't mean to scare anyone that bad," Caleb said. "We were saving the ghost for the opening night performance. But Joshua was showing me how it worked, and suddenly Mrs. Ellsworth came into the corridor when we thought everyone was rehearsing. Next thing we know, she's screaming. We hightailed it out of there too."

"The ghost was my idea," Joshua boasted. "I did a practice run that morning before anyone else was at the theater and scared Caleb half to death."

"I knew all along that ghost wasn't real," Caleb objected. "It came out of nowhere and startled me, that's all."

"Then why did you squeal like a banshee?" Joshua demanded.

Van was soon refereeing a rousing argument between the two brothers while Harriet and Ruby stood on the sidelines. Joshua teased Caleb about running through the theater shrieking at the top of his lungs, an allegation Caleb vehemently denied. Then Caleb retaliated by telling a childhood story about Joshua.

As the boys went back and forth with "yes, you did," and "no, I didn't," Van looked to Ruby for support. She responded with a huge smile, said her goodbyes, and retreated into the house.

"I guess boys will be boys," Harriet said as she and Van drove to the police station a few minutes later.

"As much trouble as they give everyone now, they're decent chaps," Van replied. "They just see the world differently than most of us."

Harriet agreed they were smart, out-of-the-box thinkers.

After they arrived at the police station, she took the stairs from the top of the bluff to the village. On her way to Joel's flat, where Will was helping him get comfortably settled, she stopped in at the

Seadog Street Deli. She chose freshly made sandwiches for lunch and also a bowl of baked potato soup for Joel to heat up and enjoy later.

When she entered the tiny flat, the two men bombarded her with the news that DI McCormick had called Joel with an update. The explosion had been caused by a small detonation device with a timer. The perpetrator either wasn't very skilled at bomb-making or had intentionally created a device that caused more noise than destruction. Most importantly, the investigative team found a couple of promising prints.

"It's Piers," Joel insisted to Harriet. He reclined on the sofa, occasionally grimacing with pain, while she and Will ate their meal at the tiny table for two in the small flat. "I know he did it, and I know he's lying about those stairs. For reasons I can't begin to understand, he's trying to sabotage me."

Harriet clung to her hope that this was a simple case of miscommunication between the two men. But would Joel ever believe that?

"Now tell us about your visit with the Corbins," Will prompted. "Did Van threaten them with tar and feathers?"

"Not even once," Harriet said, laughing. Between bites of her ham and cheese sandwich, she told them about the brothers' confessions and their pride in their technical achievements.

"Maybe I should hire them for more hauntings," Joel said. "Every respectable theater in England has a ghost. The Beacon should too."

"I imagine they'd love that," Will said. Then he squeezed Harriet's hand. "I've got news for you too. I talked to the games rental manager in Skipton. He's got a delivery to make over this way, so he's bringing Poppy the board she wanted and picking up the other one. He's waiving all delivery charges and rental fees."

A burden lifted from Harriet's shoulders that she hadn't realized was so heavy until it was gone. "That's fabulous news. Does Poppy know?"

"Yep. She'll be at the church to oversee the exchange. And so will I, and you will not."

"Thank you so much for taking care of that."

"I told you I would."

Joel coughed loudly, and they turned to him. "You two are too perfect," he said with a grin. "The best Elizabeth and Mr. Darcy I've ever directed in an amateur production."

Harriet blushed, doubting that was true, but grateful for his kind words. And that his mood had lifted.

The trio chatted a few more minutes, then Harriet and Will tidied up. As Harriet gathered her purse to leave, her phone rang.

"It's Van," she said right before she answered the call.

"Are you with Will?" he asked.

"And Joel."

"Go ahead and put me on speaker. They can hear this too."

Harriet tapped the button. "What's going on?"

"I've been trying to contact Odette," Van said. "She's not answering her phone, and she wasn't at the theater, so I drove out to the farm where she rented a room. They haven't seen her since early this morning, and all her belongings are gone."

Harriet was startled at the news. "Why would she leave? The play is only a few days away."

"That is odd." Will turned to Joel. "How well do you know her?"

"This is the first time we've worked together," he said, "though I knew her by name. She has an impeccable reputation in local arts communities throughout southern England. She contacted me when she heard I was looking for production assistants. I didn't think I could afford her, but she offered a huge discount, so I signed her on."

"Anything else you can tell me?" Van asked.

Joel adjusted a pillow and rubbed his injured leg. "When we first talked, she told me she was excited to see an old theater being brought back to life and 'wanted to be part of that story.' Plus, she already had all the costumes I needed. I'd have been a fool to say no."

"What are you going to do now?" Harriet asked Van.

"Not much I can do. She's free to go whenever and wherever she wants."

"Which is fine, as long as she didn't have anything to do with the explosion," Joel said.

"Or those threatening notes you got," Will added. "Though it seems unlikely she'd offer to help with your first production only to sabotage you."

"Unless," Harriet said slowly, "that's why she offered to help."

In between the Tuesday afternoon appointments and whenever they were out of earshot of anyone in the waiting room, Harriet and Polly talked round and round about the morning's discoveries. Despite their probing and prodding, they were no closer to answering any of their unresolved questions or solving any of the unsolved mysteries at the end of the day than they'd been at the beginning.

Their last updates came from a text to Polly from Van saying Odette still hadn't responded to any of his messages and another to Harriet from Will saying Joel insisted on keeping the next day's rehearsal schedule despite his doctor's insistence that he needed to rest.

Since Wednesday was the last day of scene rehearsals before Thursday afternoon's dress rehearsal, Harriet could understand Joel's decision. She'd probably do the same thing if she were in his director's shoes.

Once the clinic closed for the day, Harriet popped a chicken bake into the oven for a late supper. Will needed to stay longer at the church for one of Poppy's autumn bazaar meetings.

After shooing the cats outside and taking Maxwell for a walk, Harriet settled at Grandad's desk and ran her finger over his collection of leather-bound journals. If only she could remember which journal she'd been reading when she found his entries about the Kellas cat. She'd had a brief chat with Martha Banks earlier that afternoon. "Hagar seemed pleased to see me. Or at least to see her food," Martha had said with a good-hearted chuckle.

In Harriet's experience, even the most feral of cats could sometimes be wooed by a safe place to sleep and a steady diet. Many would never tolerate a human's touch, no matter how experienced or gentle, while others eventually accepted their caretaker's affection. She was interested to see where Hagar would land on that spectrum in the coming days, especially when it came time to deliver and care for her kittens.

Harriet chose a couple of likely journals and carried them into the reading nook. Maxwell trotted behind her and quickly settled in his comfy bed on the hearthrug. Charlie and Ash were already curled up together on the ottoman. She turned on the gas insert for the fireplace to remove the chill from the room and relaxed in the tall wingback chair.

Once she was settled, Harriet skimmed the first journal's pages, stopping at times to read a particular entry or prayer that Grandad had written. His faith had been as much a part of his life as his veterinary skill and his artistic talent. So often the words he'd written were exactly the ones Harriet needed to hear all these years later.

She reached the end of the first journal, opened the second, and stared at the *from* and *to* dates that Grandad had filled in on the title page. He'd written in this journal during the same weeks that Silas Hornsby fell from the balcony box and Eugenie Okehurst disappeared. Could he have written about those events?

Harriet quickly flipped through the lined pages, eager to see what Grandad might have to say about the mysterious happenings at the Beacon, and soon spotted one of the names she wanted to see.

Helen and I dressed in our Sunday best to attend a private reception at the Beacon-on-the-Moor Playhouse to meet the cast for the upcoming production of Pride and Prejudice *after their dress rehearsal. The actress who plays Elizabeth Bennet— and a fine Elizabeth she is—surprised me with a request that I paint her portrait. One of my landscapes, much to my surprise, is displayed at Sea-Holly Cottage where she's staying, and she complimented what she called my "artistic vision."*

Naturally, I declined her request, as my artistic vision rarely extends beyond rural vistas and animals to people. However, I may rue my decision should this delightful and talented young woman someday be known as Dame Eugenie Okehurst.

Harriet blinked away unexpected tears. Her grandparents had actually met Eugenie. Why hadn't that possibility occurred to her before?

Not only had they met, but it appeared Grandad and Eugenie were members of a mutual-respect society. How terrific was that? The actress certainly had good taste, that was for sure.

The next entry was written the day after Silas's accident. To Harriet's disappointment, Grandad had chosen instead to write about Ox Osman's new prize-winning bull—bought at a bargain price—that had so many of the local farmers green with jealousy.

They needn't be. He's a fine-looking specimen for sure, and worth a ribbon or two on that count alone. But I have it on good authority that his offspring are few and far between. I fear Ox has been swindled, but since he's never appreciated my advice in the past, even though kindly offered, I'll refrain from sharing my opinion on his latest acquisition. He'll find out soon enough on his own, his bragging will cease, and his neighbors' faces will return to their normal ruddy color.

Though this wasn't the story Harriet wanted to read, she still found it entertaining. Especially since she'd met no cattle farmer by that name since she'd moved to the area.

What fate had befallen Ox Osman and his famous bull? If only he'd listened to Grandad, perhaps he or his children would still have a thriving herd. At least, she'd like to think so, though it was just as likely none of his children were interested in maintaining the family farm. Having experienced the ups and downs of raising livestock and crops, not to mention the long days and—at times—even longer nights, they probably preferred an easier life for themselves and their children.

The next entries of primary interest to Harriet were extraordinarily brief.

> *October 20, 1985.*
> *Rambunctious storm. Eugenie Okehurst is missing.*

> *November 2, 1985.*
> *Gretna Green beckoned. Helen and I wish her well.*

She skimmed the next few entries and found one that caused her pulse to race.

> *November 7, 1985*
> *Why is Silas Hornsby dead?*
> *As Helen and I stood beside the other mourners at the graveside ceremony earlier today, this single question reverberated in my mind until I feared I would shout it out loud.*
> *He fell from a theater box. How?*
> *No one seems to know or has the curiosity to find out.*
> *I'm told he was seldom conscious after the incident, and when he was, he refused to answer any questions about what happened that night. Why was he silent?*

Now this amiable and good-hearted man, the best by far of the Dankworth family, is gone. The official explanation is that he succumbed to his injuries.

It's my belief that he succumbed to a broken heart.

CHAPTER TWENTY-ONE

With the dishes done and the kitchen tidied, Harriet and Will settled on the living room sofa in front of a crackling fire. After such a long and busy day, Harriet appreciated the comfort of relaxing next to her husband. Maxwell lay on the hearth, ears alert, as the cats played a rollicking game of tag. Sweet Charlie seemed to have found the mythical fountain of youth since Ash became part of the family. She and the younger cat were practically inseparable.

Harriet set her mug of chamomile tea on the side table and opened Grandad's journal to the first of the bookmarked pages. She read the entries to Will, who listened in silence until she closed the book.

"A broken heart?" Will repeated the last three words. "He didn't say any more than that? Give any kind of explanation?"

"I read all the remaining entries. He never mentions Silas again. Or Eugenie." Harriet closed the journal. "Did you know Silas was related to the Dankworths?"

Will shook his head. "Cyril and Egbert weren't mentioned in his obituary, were they?"

"It only mentioned his deceased parents and that he was an only child. Which seems so strange when Cyril lives in Whitby. He and Silas are cousins. Second cousins, to be exact."

"How do you know that?"

"Fern Chapman told me. I called her right before you came home."

"You called Fern?"

"Who else? She knows more than anyone else about local family trees." Harriet shrugged. "Besides, she's mellowed over these past months."

Will chuckled. "Maybe a little. But she's still formidable enough to play Lady Catherine de Bourgh without even acting. All she has to do is say the lines. They come out perfectly every single time."

Harriet laughed along with him. After all, he wasn't wrong. "Fern told me that the *D* in Silas D. Hornsby stands for Dankworth. Besides Cyril's family, the only other relative is their great-uncle Egbert. Cyril mentioned him when I was in the diner the other day. Remember what I told you he said?"

Will tilted his head in thought. "Something about not wanting there to be competition. We thought he must be talking about the Beacon and the Majestic. And then he said Egbert had ruined something once before and could do it again."

"Guess who owned the Beacon back then." Harriet held Will's gaze, sure he'd come up with the right answer. "Yep, Silas Hornsby."

He stared into her eyes then frowned. "You can't be serious."

"Fern told me that too." Harriet shifted her gaze to the fireplace. The flames danced among the burning logs. "Another fact left out of his obituary."

"This is crazy," Will exclaimed. "Egbert considered his own great-nephew to be so much competition that he 'ruined' the theater? We know he didn't cause the flooding, so are you suggesting—"

Will's sudden change in expression mingled disgust with deep sadness. "It's too awful to believe. His own nephew?"

"I've been thinking about this ever since I got off the phone with Fern." Harriet opened the journal again. "See what Grandad wrote here. That even when Silas was conscious, he wouldn't answer any questions. Do you think he knew what Egbert had done? Though if he did, why wouldn't he say so? I don't understand, unless it was out of some sense of misplaced family loyalty."

Will took the journal from her and read the entry for himself. "That might be a reason. But I think something even more frightening is going on here. After his fall, Silas knew Egbert was capable of doing just about anything to get what he wanted. What if Egbert threatened to hurt someone else? Someone Silas loved?"

Harriet didn't want to accept what Will was suggesting. Not even for a second. But she couldn't ignore his logic. Or the final words in Grandad's entry: *He succumbed to a broken heart.*

"The dying bachelor. The disappearing actress."

Odette's words, which Harriet now recalled she'd spoken with a significant air, came to mind.

"She said 'disappearing,' not 'eloping.'"

Will turned to her with a quizzical look. "What's that?"

"When Odette and I were talking this morning, she said she was interested in the same mysteries I am. 'The dying bachelor. The disappearing actress.' Those were her exact words." Harriet shifted in her seat and rested her knee on the cushion so she faced Will. "Why didn't she say 'eloping' actress?"

Will shrugged. "Does it matter?"

"As far as everyone else knows, Eugenie eloped."

"You're suggesting that Odette knows—for certain one hundred percent knows—she didn't?"

Harriet's imagination played out a scenario that seemed too incredible to be true yet made perfect sense. "Odette has been in the theater world a long time. She could have known Eugenie. Maybe she knew Silas too."

Odette's words echoed in Harriet's mind once more. *"The dying bachelor. The disappearing actress."*

"What if Silas loved Eugenie?" she continued. "And she was the one he wanted to protect from Egbert? And what if he couldn't?"

"Those are a lot of what-ifs and suppositions." Will pulled her into an embrace. "If you're right about any of that, then the police need to be alerted. Maybe we should look for Odette. Find out what she does and doesn't know."

"It's hard to hold out much hope Eugenie is still alive, no matter how much I wish it." Harriet released a wistful sigh. "Ever since we found out she didn't write the letter to Layla and that two men confronted her in the Crow's Nest the night she went missing, I've been afraid something awful happened to her."

She nestled deeper into Will's comforting arms. "I'd rather know the truth than wonder about her the rest of my life. Though there are still so many unanswered questions."

"We may never find out the details," Will said. "Egbert Dankworth is a shrewd old man who never leaves his house. He won't admit to anything, and all we have is supposition."

"Cyril might talk." Harriet adjusted her position so she could look into Will's eyes. "He certainly wasn't afraid for anyone to hear him spout off when he was in the diner."

"But we don't know for sure if Cyril had anything to do with Silas's fall or Eugenie's disappearance. You heard him say his uncle had ruined the Beacon—if that's what he was talking about—not that he himself had."

Harriet mulled this over, wanting desperately to find a way to hold Egbert accountable for what he'd done. Cyril too, if he was involved in any way.

The doorbell rang, and Maxwell raced as fast as his two front legs and his two back wheels could go to the foyer.

"I'll see who it is," Will volunteered. As he followed Maxwell, Harriet took the opportunity to place another log on the fire.

Will returned a moment later with their visitor.

"Piers," Harriet exclaimed, unable to hide her surprise. "How good to see you. Please, have a seat."

"Thank you." He perched on the edge of an upholstered chair.

"Would you like something to drink?" she asked. "It won't take but a minute to brew a cup of tea."

"I don't suppose I'll be here long enough for that." Piers clutched his felt hat in both hands. "There's something I have to say. It's been weighing too heavy on my shoulders to let it go on any longer."

Will sat on the end of the couch closest to Piers's chair, a relaxed smile directed at their visitor.

"If you need to talk to Will alone, I can—"

Piers shook his head. "It's best I say what I came to say to both of you. In a day or two, there won't be anyone in White Church Bay who won't know all about my troubles."

Harriet lowered herself to the raised hearth, content for Will to take the lead in a conversation she expected to turn into a confession. Her stomach knotted as she intuited the reason for Piers's visit.

He'd lied when he said he had fixed the stairs.

"I can promise you," Will said quietly, "that nothing you say in this room will be repeated unless you wish it to be."

"You're a good man, Pastor." Piers scrunched his hat even tighter. "First off, I hope you believe me when I say I didn't mean for Joel to get hurt like that. No one ever went up those steps, what with the stairwell being locked and all."

Piers hung his head, and his shoulders shook. When he'd composed himself, he straightened his posture and looked directly at Will.

"The last year has been a hard one. My sister's husband got hit by a lorry and hasn't been able to work, so he lost his job. Then my sister got sick, and the doctors can't seem to decide on what's wrong. She lost her job too. It's been one hard-luck thing after another for them."

"I'm so sorry to hear that." Will leaned forward as he focused his attention on Piers.

"There's supposed to be a settlement coming from the lorry company," Piers went on. "But there's one delay after another. I've been filling in the gaps best I can so they don't lose their house. It's been hard, and I never meant anyone to get hurt."

He looked so forlorn that Harriet could hardly stand it. She wished she knew the best way to help him.

"Why don't you tell me what happened?" Will prompted in his gentle pastoral tone.

"When Joel gave me the contract to fix up the Beacon, I felt God had answered my prayers. It surely did help there for a while. But then another bill came up and another and another. They needed money I didn't have to give them. I thought if I could cause a little leak in the plumbing and Joel had me come in to fix it, then I'd have a bit extra to send my sister. And once I did that, the next time was easier. And then the time after that."

Though Harriet sympathized with Piers's plight, his solution made her feel sick to her stomach. Joel's suspicions had been right. Piers purposely caused problems and then repaired them. Had he done something similar when he worked on her home? Or to any of the other customers who'd placed their trust in his expertise?

"About a week ago I vowed to never do it again, but then my sister called with another emergency. Joel once said no one would be going up those steps for months. I gave him an invoice saying the work was already done so he'd go ahead and write me a check. If I'd had any notion he'd decide to go up to that second level, I never would have lied like I did. My conscience has been bothering me something terrible ever since."

"That's because you're a good man." Will said. "And you know that when we confess our wrongdoings, God forgives us."

Harriet closed her eyes and breathed a silent prayer. Poor Piers. He'd spent his entire working life building up his reputation and goodwill with his customers. All that could come crashing down because he wanted to help his family.

"I wish I didn't have to ask you this." Will waited for Piers to give him his full attention. "Did you have anything to do with Saturday's explosion?"

Piers's face turned a thousand shades of red.

"The police know it wasn't an accident," Will added, "and they found evidence left by the culprit."

"I had nothing to do with that. Honest, Pastor. I've just confessed to all I did, and I'll confess to Joel too. But that explosion had nothing to do with me nor me with it." Once again, he hung his head, kneading his hat with his thick fingers. "That wasn't me."

Harriet caught Will's gaze. "I'll fix tea," she said quietly, and he nodded agreement.

Once in the kitchen, she filled the kettle with water. Her mind whirled with all the revelations the day had unexpectedly provided. Not only because of the Corbin boys admitting to creating the ghost and DI McCormick's phone call to Joel with news of the explosion, but also thanks to Odette and a few entries in Grandad's journal.

But for now, Harriet's primary concern centered on finding out who had written the threatening notes to Joel and who had caused the explosion.

Harriet suspected there was only one answer. But proving Cyril Dankworth and his great-uncle were the culprits wouldn't be easy. Especially with the opening-night performance only a few days away.

If the Dankworths were intent on ruining the Beacon, what might they do on that important evening to stop the show?

CHAPTER TWENTY-TWO

Thick fog rolled in from the sea early Wednesday morning and clung to the cliffs with a tenacity rarely associated with ethereal mists. On days like today, Harriet was especially thankful that her workplace was on the other side of the kitchen door instead of in the village or Whitby. Barring any emergencies, her workload promised to be a light one with only a few appointments on the schedule and a short list of follow-up calls.

The afternoon and perhaps most of the evening would be spent at the theater for the final rehearsals before tomorrow afternoon's dress rehearsal. Harriet had already heard on the very efficient White Church Bay grapevine that Joel asked Ruby to step into Odette's giant shoes. Harriet heard she was nervous about taking on the responsibility but that everyone agreed she was the obvious choice, since she'd already been working with the cast's costumes.

Harriet's cinnamon bagel popped up from the toaster, and she topped it with an apple-walnut cream cheese. Will had left a few minutes earlier, a to-go cup of Earl Grey laced with honey in one hand and his messenger bag in the other. She'd said a quick prayer for him then and said another one for him now.

After Piers's confession the night before, Will had guided him into creating a restitution plan that included meetings with Van and

Joel. It would be up to those two to decide on any criminal charges or civil lawsuits. Piers claimed he was prepared to face any consequences for his actions, no matter how dire, though he also feared being blamed for the explosion.

Before he left to pick up Piers, Will told Harriet that he hoped Piers's sister and her husband weren't taking advantage of his generosity. As Will walked out the door, Harriet had prayed God would give him wisdom and grant Piers mercy and grace.

Now, while enjoying her bagel, Harriet opened her laptop and went online to purchase a few household staples. She reached into her sling bag for her wallet that held her credit card but pulled out a vintage wallet instead.

The one she'd found in her vanity drawer yesterday morning.

She immediately chided herself for forgetting something so important then quickly put a stop to that nonsense. Why would she remember it with everything else that had happened yesterday? From meeting with Piers at the theater first thing in the morning to meeting with him again here at their home last thing at night, the entire day had been incredibly busy and all-around exhausting. By the time she went to sleep, she'd been physically, mentally, and emotionally drained.

Since Polly wasn't scheduled to work in the clinic today, Harriet only had about fifteen more minutes before she unlocked the doors. She quickly finished with her purchase then turned her attention to Eugenie's wallet.

She'd examined the driver's license when she first opened the wallet but had only glanced at the photos before she went in search of Will. And ended up in that strange conversation with Odette.

The first photo showed Eugenie, dressed in an eighteenth-century costume, standing in front of a backdrop displaying a huge estate. The words *Pride and Prejudice* were emblazoned across the top. The young woman standing next to her wore a vibrant pink knee-length dress with a flared skirt and matching high heels. Judging from their huge smiles and sparkling expressions, the photo captured a very special occasion. The opening of the show, perhaps? Or the end of a successful run?

Harriet turned the sleeve and read the words written on the other side of the photo: *Layla and me as Lydia. Plymouth Globe. March 1985.*

Eugenie had once played Lydia? Given the parallels between Lydia's story and Eugenie's supposed elopement, that somehow seemed fitting.

Harriet flipped the photo back over. "So you're Layla Hastings. The apprentice seamstress who lied about receiving a letter from Eugenie. Why would you do that to your friend?"

There were a couple of plausible explanations. If—and it was admittedly a big *if*—Silas stayed silent because he was frightened of his uncle, then maybe Layla had produced the letter for the same reason. Perhaps she didn't want Egbert to know she knew the truth.

Whatever that truth might be.

Harriet sighed in frustration. Both she and Will were certain Egbert had deliberately injured Silas and done something nefarious to Eugenie, which was why Grandad believed Silas died of a broken heart. But they didn't know the details and probably never would unless Egbert decided to break his forty years of silence. A very unlikely scenario. Harriet doubted Van could get the great-uncle to answer any questions, not even if he confronted him with evidence that someone had tampered with the balcony. Why would he? That evidence wasn't very strong—not after all these years—and there was no proof Egbert had anything to do with it.

Another possible explanation for Layla's lie was that she'd written the letter so authorities would stop looking for Eugenie. If that was her motive, then her plan had succeeded. The next logical question, however, was a simple *why*.

Did Layla know Eugenie would never be found alive? Was she responsible for Eugenie's disappearance? Or had she been in league with Egbert? More questions that might never be answered unless Layla could be found. Since Colleen, with all her expertise, hadn't located any online information about Layla, Harriet didn't hold out much hope for ever learning the truth.

The second photo, separated from the first by a few empty sleeves, showed Eugenie and a young man sitting on what looked like a park bench. Harriet turned the sleeve over in hopes of finding out the young man was Silas Hornsby. The words on the back read: *My true Mr. Darcy.*

No location. No date.

No name.

Frowning with disappointment, Harriet flipped the photo back over. The sandy-haired man's chiseled features and light-colored eyes suggested a Scandinavian heritage. He appeared to be in his early to midtwenties and, from the expression on his handsome face, very much in love with the actress tucked into his side.

And also, somehow familiar. She must have seen a photo of this man before, but where? She reached for her Beacon/Okehurst folder and sorted through the pages till she found what she was looking for—Silas's obituary.

She'd paid little attention to the grainy black-and-white photo when she first read the creatively written announcement. As soon as she pulled it from the folder, though, she recognized Silas as the man in Eugenie's photo. Proof that the "dying bachelor" and the "disappearing actress" had been in love.

The confirmation squeezed Harriet's heart until it hurt. Had they planned an elopement that was thwarted by Silas's fall? Or was the idea of an elopement only a product of Layla's imagination? One inspired by a Jane Austen novel and a stage play?

Unfortunately, in a court of law, the photo proved nothing.

Harriet longed to learn something—anything—that would provide enough probable cause for Silas's incident to be reopened and Egbert to be interrogated. Or, if she and Will were wrong, something that would prove his innocence.

She placed the photo from the obituary next to the photo in its wallet sleeve. The former was a formal headshot, which she supposed was used for professional purposes. Though the quality wasn't very good—this was a printout of a newspaper article, after all—the side-by-side comparison contrasted a serious demeanor with a more playful one.

As she studied the obituary photo, she was struck again with the feeling of familiarity. Perhaps it was the tilt of Silas's head or the distant expression in his eyes. Harriet couldn't say for sure. But Silas reminded her of something other than another photo of himself.

The kitchen clock chimed, and Harriet startled. She needed to put all thoughts of Silas and Eugenie aside and focus on her patients.

Her attention was caught once again by the couple's photo as she started to close the wallet.

And then she had an idea.

One aspect of Joel's marketing for the theater's grand opening was his deliberate choice for *Pride and Prejudice* to be its first production. In that way, the theater's present and future was tied to its past.

The promotional materials included images of the 1980s playbill juxtaposed against the current version and a professional photograph of the historic theater.

What if the wallet-sized photo of the Beacon's former owner with his arm around P&P's leading actress was blown up to poster size and displayed in the theater lobby? One of the reporters from the *Whitby Gazette* might be persuaded to write a story about their secret romance.

Harriet's heart started racing.

A secret from the general public, perhaps, but what about Silas's great-uncle Egbert? How upset would he be if the photo became public? Might he—or Cyril on his behalf—protest too much? And, fingers crossed, accidentally incriminate himself?

Harriet latched the wallet and was about to return it to her sling bag when she was struck by its thickness. She'd had a similar wallet once that thickened when she carried several bills, but this wallet's bills compartment was empty. Still, something seemed odd.

Even as she told herself that she was imagining things, she examined the wallet again and with extra care. Soon she discovered a hidden slot cleverly located behind the bills compartment and accessed from the bottom edge instead of along the top. When Harriet slipped her fingers into the space, she felt stiff paper.

A hidden cache of cash?

Her heart raced with anticipation as she tugged at the find. At first, the paper seemed stuck, but she slowly worked it out of its hiding spot. Her heart beat even faster as she opened a 5x7 photo that had been folded lengthwise. She stared in disbelief at what she held in her hands.

The picture, a close-up, showed Eugenie and Silas holding a document. Harriet hurriedly rummaged through a drawer for a magnifying glass to confirm she was reading what she thought she was reading.

The Gretna Green marriage license stated that Silas Dankworth Hornsby and Eugenie Amelia Okehurst were wed on August 1, 1985.

More than two months before Silas's fall.

CHAPTER TWENTY-THREE

When Harriet and Will were chosen for their roles in *Pride and Prejudice*, Harriet had marked all the various rehearsals on the calendar and declared Thursday, the night of the dress rehearsal, and Friday, the first performance, as office holidays. She'd expected both days would be hectic and wanted them as free from other obligations as possible.

The early morning discovery of the marriage license, however, threatened to upend that plan.

Over a simple lunch of sandwich wraps and pasta salads, Harriet and her trustworthy coconspirators—Will, Polly, and Van—launched Operation P&P. They all agreed that the secret marriage deepened their suspicions that Silas's fall was no accident and heightened their concerns about Eugenie's disappearance.

Considering Silas had still been alive, though unconscious in the hospital, it seemed odd that none of the notes on Eugenie's missing person's report mentioned any connection between her and her secret husband. If any of the other Stanhope Players knew of the marriage, they kept the information to themselves. Even Layla, Eugenie's supposed best friend, either didn't know or kept her mouth shut.

Why?

That question came up again and again as the four discussed various *what-ifs* and *how abouts*.

"I gave Fern another call," Harriet told the others when the conversation turned to Egbert Dankworth. The Chapman family traced their roots in the Yorkshire moors into previous centuries, and Fern was a walking encyclopedia when it came to the histories of the area's oldest families.

"Did you tell her about the photo?" Polly asked as she speared a corkscrew pasta.

"No, though I had to promise to 'tell all' over tea in the next week or so." Not that Harriet minded. A little bit of Fern, who was in her mid- to late-fifties could go a long way, but Harriet had come to appreciate her eccentricities and plain-speaking. And her proven ability to keep important secrets.

"She told me that Egbert doted on Cyril and not so much on Silas, who was about ten years younger."

Van held up his hand. "Let me guess why. Because Cyril was a Dankworth and Silas wasn't."

"A gold star for you," Harriet quipped. "The Dankworth tree is, in Fern's words, 'skinnier than a Lombardy poplar' these days, and Egbert insisted that his nephews remain in a specific social sphere."

"One that wouldn't include a Stanhope Players actress," Will said.

"Which could explain why the newlyweds kept their secret." Harriet sighed as a wave of sadness washed over her. "I can't imagine how Eugenie maintained her sanity. She must have been worried sick about Silas."

Polly set her fork down and swiped her fingers on a napkin. "I have to believe she snuck into the hospital to see him. In the middle of the night when hardly anyone else was around. Nothing could have kept me from Van when he was hospitalized. Not even a scary uncle."

Van squeezed Polly's hand. "A scary uncle who may have retaliated by tossing his nephew over a balcony. Though I doubt he did it himself."

"Fern said he's a shady character despite all his 'lordly pretensions,'" Harriet said. "Again, her words."

"I've been thinking," Will said. "Whether or not Egbert knew of the marriage back then, I can't imagine he'd be pleased even now for people to know about Silas and Eugenie's elopement. In fact, I think that photo of the marriage license could cause him to lose his temper."

"And maybe do something foolish?" Van ventured. "Maybe even incriminating?"

Since the date on the marriage license conflicted with the story that Eugenie had eloped with a mysterious groom after her disappearance, Harriet hoped that DI McCormick would consider reopening both Silas's and Eugenie's cases.

After all, Silas might have been the victim of attempted murder. And Eugenie's missing person's case had never been solved. She most certainly hadn't eloped to Gretna Green with some other man, so where had she gone instead? And why had she never shown up anywhere else again?

By the time lunch was over, the two couples had devised a plan for finding the answers to their questions. Operation P&P was a go, and each agent had an assignment.

Within a few hours, Van confirmed with officials in Scotland that the Hornsby-Okehurst marriage license was legitimate. He paid the fee for a certified copy to be delivered to him the next day.

Will enlisted Piers, whose legal fate was still being decided, to construct a special case to display the license. Polly designed and distributed flyers for local merchants to display about a surprise announcement to be made during the intermission of Friday night's performance of *Pride and Prejudice*.

During a midafternoon break, Harriet arranged a Thursday morning appointment with Colleen at the *Gazette* to talk about an ad for the newspaper's special edition covering the Beacon's grand opening and the production's preparations.

Just as she finished making the arrangements with Colleen, Harriet's phone beeped. It was Will, calling with the news that his dad was arriving the next day to attend the dress rehearsal.

"He's wants to take us to tea," Will said. "Does four o'clock work for you? We can meet him at the White Hart."

So much for keeping Thursday free, though Harriet was thrilled beyond words to add the tea to her calendar. She'd only met Will's father face-to-face once before, at their wedding, and welcomed the opportunity to spend more time with him.

After the call ended with Will and in between seeing to her patients, Harriet focused on her other preparations for the part she needed to play in Operation P&P.

CHAPTER TWENTY-FOUR

The day of the dress rehearsal had finally arrived. Harriet awoke with the butterflies in her stomach already performing aerodynamic acrobatics that defied description. How was she ever supposed to make it through this overly scheduled Thursday?

An hour or so later, she sat beside Colleen at a table in the *Gazette* office, staring at a huge monitor that displayed a mock-up of Friday's special edition. After hearing what Harriet had in mind, Colleen had convinced the editor to give her space in the coveted above-the-fold area.

Harriet wished she could have told Colleen the "rest of the story," but that would have to wait until the whole truth came out. If it ever did.

Bile threatened to rise in Harriet's stomach at the thought that they might be going to so much effort for nothing. But it was a risk she was willing to take. They'd talked it over yesterday as they'd fine-tuned their plan, and Will, Polly, and Van felt the same way.

"I have to tell you again," Colleen said as she manipulated images on the screen, "how glad I am you found these photos. This is exactly the kind of human-interest story that captures the imagination. It's got everything. Romance. Drama. Tragedy."

Everything but an ending.

But Harriet couldn't say that. Not even when Colleen commented that the photo made it unlikely that Eugenie had eloped with someone else. Hopefully others would ask themselves similar questions about her disappearance.

Harriet stared at the monitor, entranced, as the photo of Eugenie and Silas snapped into place below a headline that read: A PRIDE AND PREJUDICE TRUE-LIFE LOVE STORY. The accompanying fluff piece suggested, but refrained from stating as fact, that the P&P star and Beacon theater owner were romantically involved.

The article's tone was in keeping with the entire four-page special edition, which included interviews with the amateur cast members, a write-up featuring Joel, behind-the-scene anecdotes, and even an op-ed titled: IS THE BEACON ENGLAND'S NEXT HAUNTED THEATER?

Colleen typed in the caption for the photo then leaned back in her chair. "Voilà! What do you think?"

"It's eye-catching," Harriet responded. Exactly as she'd hoped it would be. "They're an attractive couple."

"Are we sure Silas is related to Cyril Dankworth?" Colleen joked though she'd already confirmed through a public records search that they were. She inserted the grainy obituary photo into its intended spot. "Cyril resembles his great-uncle enough for them to be twins born decades apart, but not Silas."

Harriet turned to Colleen, puzzled. "How do you know what Egbert looked like when he was Cyril's age?"

"I've seen old photographs of Egbert in the archives. If not for the date and changes in fashion, you'd think you were looking at Cyril."

Colleen worked at editing Silas's obituary image so that it appeared sharper than the original grainy photo. The woman was definitely multi-skilled and a huge asset to the newspaper. "Perfect," she cheerfully declared.

Harriet agreed.

This article, a brief bio on Silas as the former owner of the Beacon-on-the-Moor Playhouse, was below the fold and positioned next to the article on Joel as the current owner. A bold "Now and Then" headline stretched across both articles and above their separate headlines.

Harriet skimmed the articles then focused her attention on the photographs. Joel's photo, like Silas's, was a professional black-and-white headshot. She stretched out her fingers as if to touch the photos then drew back her hand.

"Are you seeing what I'm seeing?" she asked Colleen.

"If you mean their resemblance to each other, yes. Are they related?"

"I don't know." Harriet couldn't stop staring at the photographs. Both men had the same eyes and nose, but Silas had a stronger jaw. And more hair, but of course he was younger in his photo than Joel was in his.

"It's disconcerting to see the photos so close together," she said. "Especially when Silas, if he were still alive, would be at least twenty years older than Joel."

"More like twenty-five," Colleen said. "Joel's article says he's thirty-nine. He was born a few months after Silas died."

Harriet's mind raced as she fit this astonishing information into what she already knew…and what she'd thought she knew.

Since Silas and Eugenie were married and it was possible Silas could be Joel's father, then that meant Eugenie might be his mother.

That would mean she hadn't run off to Gretna Green to elope like everyone was led to believe. Eugenie might have left White Church Bay to protect her unborn child from the man she suspected of fatally injuring her husband.

And that brought Harriet full circle to the question she'd started with when she first learned of Eugenie's disappearance.

Where was the actress now?

***

"You can't stay here at the inn when we have a perfectly suitable guest room waiting for you," Harriet said to Will's dad.

"Now ye didn't go to no trouble, did ye, lass?" Gordon responded in his thick Scottish brogue. "That's why I came close to surprising you at the theater tonight instead of letting you know ahead of time I was coming."

"It's still a nice surprise to have you here. But we'll get to see more of you if you stay with us." Harriet turned to her husband. "Please convince him."

"You heard her, Dad. It'll be great."

"Then I suppose you've talked me into it." Gordon's jovial laugh never failed to make Harriet smile. This surprise visit might just be the tonic she needed to calm her nerves before tonight's dress rehearsal. Though the rehearsal was no longer the only event that had her heart jumping.

After their waiter brought their order of assorted sandwiches and cakes along with a pot of cinnamon tea, Will asked his dad about the train trip from Scotland.

His parents had moved from Muckle Roe, one of the Shetland Islands, to White Church Bay before Will was born. They'd lived in a small cottage on the moors where Will had, by all accounts, been given the blessing of an idyllic childhood.

Sadly, his mother died shortly before Will was ordained. Not long after, his dad decided to return to his Muckle Roe roots. Then Will returned to his childhood home as the pastor of White Church after serving for a short time at the small two-church charge in Foxglove End.

After catching up on news about mutual friends, Gordon laid down his fork. "Here's some news I've been meaning to tell you. Do you remember that elderly gentleman I met a while back? We've been getting together every so often, and it turns out he's interested in genealogy. Same as me."

"I remember," Will replied. "It sounded like he was lonely and in need of a friend."

"That's the one. Anyway, we've been comparing notes, and it looks like we're distantly related. Though we're not sure yet exactly how the trees fit together, we're trying to figure it out."

"I want to see that tree when you're done with it," Will said.

As they were enjoying the last of their tea, Poppy appeared in the doorway then made a beeline to their table. Without even thinking, Harriet sent Will a "not-again" look, which his dad must have also caught and correctly interpreted. He eyed Poppy as he leaned back in his chair, a discerning expression on his face.

"I didn't expect to find you here of all places," Poppy said to Harriet. "But I'm glad, since I need your help with the autumn bazaar."

Gordon stood with the bearing of an aristocrat and pulled out the fourth chair. "Please, have a seat. You're Poppy Schofield, aren't you? The baker of delicious delicacies at the Biscuit Bistro?"

Poppy's cheeks flushed. "Why, yes. That's me." She lowered herself into the chair. "I must have left my manners outside the door, rushing in here the way I did. You see, I was passing by, and there was Harriet's vehicle in the car park. That reminded me of a little task I need doing."

"Am I to understand you're in charge of the autumn bazaar?" Gordon appeared suitably impressed. "What a tremendous responsibility you have on your shoulders. All while managing a very successful business."

"I don't mind the work," Poppy said. "Not when it's for such a good cause."

"That it is. I remember Bonnie—Will's mother, that is—baking and sewing and knitting when she was on the different church committees. She had the temperament and the personality for that kind of thing, she did, the same as you. God gives us all the gifts we need to fulfill His plans, don't you agree?"

"Why, yes. I do."

"Take our Harriet," he continued. "She has a God-given gift too, don't you know. Tending to His creatures and making them well again when she can. Comforting those that loved them when she can't. And it's all well and good for her to do a little baking or decorating now and again on a committee here or there. But I do hope that the good women of this church appreciate what she does and understand what her true calling is."

Poppy simply stared at Gordon, her eyes wide open and her mouth agape. Harriet, feeling slightly embarrassed, wanted to say something to smooth over any hurt feelings, but Will gripped her hand and gave her a smile that said everything was going to be okay.

"We do understand," Poppy said when she finally found her voice. She directed a huge smile at Gordon. "I can personally assure you that we are all so proud of our pastor's wife. Even though I don't have a pet myself, those who do think so highly of Harriet. As do the farmers hereabouts."

"I'm happy to know that's so." Gordon leaned closer. "You were saying you needed help. Is there a task or an errand I could do for you? Harriet and Will need to prepare for this evening's dress rehearsal, you see, so I came to do what I can to pitch in and then watch the play."

Poppy's cheeks flushed. "It's nothing that can't wait until another day. Though I do have something you might be interested in seeing." She rummaged through her handbag and drew out one of Polly's flyers. "As if the play wasn't exciting enough, now there's this. I'll leave it with you, as I must be going."

Poppy stood, and Gordon rose alongside her. "Such a gentleman," she said with a giggle. "And such a pleasure to see you again. Stop by the Bistro while you're visiting, and I'll make sure you get an extra special pastry."

"I will surely do that."

With a last finger wave in Harriet's direction, Poppy scurried out the door.

Harriet let out an astonished breath then turned to Will. "Did you tell your dad?"

"I have eyes, don't I?" Gordon said before Will could respond. "And I've been on this earth a good long while. Certainly long enough to know the expectations that can be put on a pastor's wife. I only hope I've eased the burden a little."

Will chuckled. "You got her out of being asked to do at least one job. I'll count that as a victory."

"And I'm immensely grateful," Harriet added. She could see that Gordon's approach of laying out the truth for Poppy had gotten through to her, finally. That same method of setting boundaries, without accusing, might serve her well in the future.

Gordon picked up the flyer that Poppy had left on the table and read it. "Now tell me, what's this all about? Or do I need to wait until tomorrow night's intermission too?"

"We're trying to prod a bear," Will said, lowering his voice. "We'll have to tell you the rest later."

"I'm even more intrigued."

Harriet shared a smile with Will. Her insides were jumpy, and not only because of dress rehearsal jitters. Egbert Dankworth might rage in his own home when he found out what they'd discovered, but that didn't mean he'd confess to anything.

Something else concerned her even more.

When Gordon stopped to chat with an acquaintance, Harriet drew Will aside to a quiet corner.

"Tell me again what you know about Joel's family," she said.

"His parents died in a car accident when he was a teen. After that, he was in and out of foster homes."

"His adoptive parents died, right?" Harriet took a deep breath. "I think I know who his birth parents were."

Will's eyes got big. "You do?"

"Not without a birth certificate or a DNA test. But look at this." She slid a printout that Colleen had given her of Joel's photo next to Silas's photo. "This will be in tomorrow's special edition of the *Gazette*."

"Wow. He looks more like Silas than I look like my dad." Will blew out a breath. "Can I keep this? Joel needs to see it before everyone else in the village does."

"You should talk to him after the rehearsal."

"Agreed," Will said. "I wonder if Egbert subscribes to the *Gazette*."

"I wonder if he already knows."

If he caused so much harm to his own great-nephew, what would he try to do to Joel for the crime of being born?

CHAPTER TWENTY-FIVE

Harriet could barely breathe as the second act of Friday night's opening performance drew to a close with the news reaching the Bennet family of Lydia's foolhardy elopement with George Wickham. Though she'd managed to stay focused on her role throughout the first two acts—to *be* Elizabeth as much as her limited talents would allow—other thoughts now intruded.

How could she not think about Eugenie being on this same stage forty years ago? How could she not look up at the broken railing on Silas Hornsby's reserved box and not be aware that this was the moment in the play when he fell?

From her vantage point in the wings, she could observe Cyril Dankworth seated in the VIP section of the auditorium along with a woman Harriet assumed was his wife. Did she know about the harm her husband and his great-uncle had caused? Did he realize that DI McCormick was seated only a row behind him for a reason?

Harriet had experienced a few twinges of guilt during the past couple of days when her suspicions of Egbert for crimes he might not have committed wavered. Or when she thought about how she might be blaming Cyril for his childish notes and the explosion when she had no solid proof.

Even though the very American principle of "innocent until proven guilty" was deeply ingrained into Harriet's consciousness, she'd made an exception when it came to the malevolent uncle and his loudmouth nephew.

Though she still wasn't certain Egbert caused Silas to fall or had injured Eugenie in any way, the same couldn't be said for Cyril.

Only an hour before the curtain was to rise, DI McCormick had received the report that proved Cyril planted the device that caused the explosion. The fingerprints on the device matched a print they found on one of Joel's notes. Since Cyril had served a short stint in the military, the forensic tech was able to make the match. She'd also received confirmation of an incriminating text message thread found in Cyril's phone records dated the evening of the explosion that was between him and his great-uncle.

Police officers were at the Dankworth estate that very moment to bring Egbert in for questioning. He might, with the help of his defense attorney, escape justice and live out the rest of his days in freedom. But Cyril would soon face the consequences of his actions. The threatening notes might not be a serious crime, but his punishment for destruction of property would be decided by the legal system.

The curtain fell on the second act, but the auditorium lights didn't rise, and no one moved from their seat. Intrigued by the flyers that had been circulated yesterday, the audience was obviously eager to hear the promised special announcement.

Harriet entered from the left wing as Joel entered from the right. They met in the middle, where Joshua had placed a small lectern a moment before. Joel spoke a few words of welcome then introduced Harriet.

"I'm sure most of you have seen today's special edition of the *Whitby Gazette*," she said. "You've read about Eugenie Okehurst's disappearance and Silas Hornsby's mysterious fall from that balcony box."

As Harriet glanced at Cyril, who squirmed in his seat, Caleb shone a spotlight on the broken railing for all to see. Some sitting in the seats beneath the box laughed nervously. If the show hadn't been sold out, Harriet was certain several of them would move.

Joel took up the threads of the story. "Way back then, when police read a letter supposedly written by Eugenie to her friend, Layla Hastings, they stopped searching for her. Eugenie told Layla that she'd eloped, but she didn't identify her bridegroom."

"We now know that Eugenie didn't write that letter," Harriet added. "But she did get married in Gretna Green."

Joel took a deep breath before speaking. Harriet couldn't imagine how hard it must be for him to tell this story, knowing as he now did that it wasn't about two star-crossed lovers but his own parents. Will had volunteered to take his place, but Joel wanted to be the one on the stage, no matter how difficult it might be to keep control of his emotions. His part of the story wouldn't be told tonight though. Joel wanted to be one hundred percent sure first.

"Eugenie eloped and was married on August 1, 1985, two and a half months before her disappearance from White Church Bay. I have the proof right here." Joel lifted the marriage license, which was now in a gold-rimmed frame.

"The name of the man she married?" He paused, not only for dramatic effect but to glare at his father's cousin. "That man was Silas Hornsby."

"Liar!" Cyril jumped to his feet. "You're nothing but a thieving liar. Great-uncle Egbert told me who you are."

As Cyril pushed his way to the end of his row, DI McCormick rose to her feet and met him in the aisle with a set of handcuffs. Sergeant Oduba, who'd been standing at the side of the stage, joined her.

The audience erupted in gasps and excited chatter, and the inspector clicked the cuffs in place. Cyril grumbled and spouted as DI McCormick and Sergeant Oduba escorted him up the aisle and into the lobby where other police officers waited to take him to the Whitby jail.

Harriet exchanged a smile with Joel, whose facial expression exhibited deep satisfaction while an equally deep sadness glistened in his eyes. Then she slipped through the curtains. After all that excitement, she needed a moment to compose herself before changing her costume for her next scene. She sat at the table located near the stage-left wing, closed her eyes, and massaged her forehead.

A moment later, she sensed someone standing nearby. She opened her eyes.

"Aunt Jinny!" She jumped up and embraced her beloved aunt in a tight hug. "I've missed you so much."

"And I've missed you." Aunt Jinny stepped back then squeezed Harriet's hands. She gazed at her with a radiant smile. "You look absolutely gorgeous. The perfect Elizabeth."

"I don't know about that," Harriet said. "What are you doing here?"

"Surely you didn't think I'd miss my niece's theatrical debut, did you?" Aunt Jinny tilted her head and pretended to give Harriet a stern look. "We've obviously got a lot of catching up to do."

"I can't wait." She pulled her aunt into another hug.

The sound of someone clearing her throat drew both women's attention to the wing. Poppy stepped onto the stage with her shoulders bowed and a dismal expression on her face. "I'm sorry to interrupt your homecoming, Jinny. But I hoped to have a word with Harriet before my courage fails me."

Aunt Jinny shifted her gaze from Poppy to Harriet and back again. "That sounds serious." She squeezed Harriet's hand. "I'll find you after the show," she promised.

"Come to my dressing room."

"Will do." With a final smile directed to both Harriet and Poppy, Aunt Jinny left them alone.

Harriet mentally braced herself for whatever Poppy had come there to say. But Poppy didn't say anything. Just bit her lip and blinked her eyes.

"I don't have much time," Harriet finally said.

Poppy scrunched her nose as a torrent of words poured from her lips. "I can't stop thinking about what Gordon said and he was such a gentleman and so very kind and I know he's right, that you're so busy already and I don't know why I kept bugging you to do this and that when others depend on you too, and you're a newlywed, and then it hit me that I'm jealous because you can do so much and I can do so little."

When she paused to take a breath, Harriet started to protest, but Poppy held up a hand to stop her.

"So I thought about what Gordon said again," she continued, though no longer in a rush to get all her words out in one fell swoop. "And it's true that I was feeling jealous, but there's no need for that. Because it's not true that you do 'much' and I do 'little.' We do 'different.' Will you please forgive me for piling burdens on your shoulders that you didn't need to carry?"

Harriet blinked back tears as Poppy neared the end of her speech. The woman had been a pebble in Harriet's shoe in recent weeks, but there were so many other weeks and months when she'd shown kindness and generosity and a willingness to step in and step up.

"I forgive you," Harriet said, holding out her arms. "I'm grateful to have you as a friend."

Despite the buzz of activity and gossip during intermission, the curtain rose on the third act on schedule, and the actors did a phenomenal job performing their roles, if Harriet did say so herself. When the final curtain dropped, the cast members were given a standing ovation, and so was Joel when he joined them on stage.

Harriet was enjoying a glass of celebratory punch when she received a text from an unknown number.

MEET ME WHERE WE TALKED BEFORE. IN THE CROSSOVER ALCOVE.

Odette!

Harriet hurriedly made her way to the alcove and found the costume designer, dressed in gray and black, perched on the trunk in the corner.

"Why did you leave?" Harriet asked. "And why are you here now?"

"Perhaps some secrets should stay that way. No matter how much one plans, one cannot foresee all possible outcomes. Or if what is intended for good will turn out for ill."

"You've said that to me before."

"It's as true now as it was then." Odette lowered her eyes a moment and clasped her hands. When she met Harriet's gaze again, a tear shimmered on her cheek. "You are good at solving mysteries. Thank you for bringing peace where there has been so much turmoil. Even if the Dankworths don't go to jail, at least their reputations have been tarnished."

"I still have questions. Layla's letter for instance. Eugenie didn't write it."

Odette pressed her lips into an amused smile. "After Silas's so-called accident, Eugenie realized her life was in danger, and that of her unborn child. The letter was a ruse. However, Layla accidentally spilled tea on the original, so she had to write it again."

"How do you know all this?" As soon as she asked the question, Harriet gasped. "You're Eugenie."

"No, my dear Harriet. Eugenie died a few days after Joel was born." Odette leaned forward. "We were the best of friends, Eugenie and me."

"You're Layla?"

"Silas knew Egbert would never accept his marriage or a Hornsby inheriting the Dankworth estate." Her lips curved into a mischievous smile. "He's still holding out hope that Cyril will have a child, though that seems unlikely after all these years."

"Why did he care so much?"

Odette shrugged. "He's always been a twisted, angry, and cruel man who longs to return to the days of aristocratic rule. And he wasn't above causing bodily harm to punish anyone who crossed him."

"Did he mean for Silas to die?"

"Only he knows." She tapped Harriet's arm. "We made a plan—Eugenie, Silas, and me. If any harm came to Silas, she was to flee. But instead of going to Gretna Green, she found refuge with a maiden aunt of mine who lived in a remote corner of Cornwall. There she had her son, and there she died."

Tears glistened on Odette's brown cheeks. "I kept her wallet, so she only had a fake ID with her when she traveled. And I arranged for Joel's adoption with an excellent family. But I suppose you know how that turned out."

"I do."

"You have so many questions, I know. I wish I could stay and answer them all." She smiled her enigmatic smile then glanced toward the door. "Do I hear your husband calling?"

"I don't think so." Harriet stepped to the door and looked along the corridor. Will was nowhere to be seen. "He's not there," she said as she turned around. "What about those men—"

The alcove was empty except for a folder lying on the trunk. Harriet opened it and glanced through the pages. Joel's birth certificate. Copies of Silas Hornsby's and Eugenie Okehurst Hornsby's wills. A sealed envelope addressed to Joel in Odette's handwriting. A few other documents relating to finances and property.

Holding the folder close, Harriet stood in the silence for a moment then took the stairs to the stage-left wings. The sounds of the celebration filtered from the lobby into the dim auditorium.

Though she was missing the party, Harriet needed this quiet moment of solitude. She strolled across the front of the stage and gazed at the balcony box.

Two shadows moved, shifted, then stepped forward. An ethereal sandy-haired man with handsome features and his arm around a classic girl-next-door beauty.

They faded away, and two lanky teens with huge grins on their faces took their place.

Harriet laughed as she returned the Corbin brothers' waves.

FROM THE AUTHOR

Dear Reader,

Who among us hasn't dealt with a Pushy Poppy? Or been weighed down by unrealistic expectations?

That little word *no* can be amazingly difficult to say sometimes, even when we *know* it needs to be said.

In this story, Will's dad affirms Poppy's God-given gifts and contrasts them with Harriet's calling. These are the gifts, given by God, that these women "received to serve others, as faithful stewards of God's grace in its various forms" (1 Peter 4:10; NIV). These are the gifts we need to nurture so that when opportunities arise to serve others, we can say *yes*.

Here's a caveat. Sometimes God calls us to do something we don't feel capable of doing. Sometimes a pressing need requires an immediate sacrifice of our time and resources.

We should be sensitive to those exceptions, of course. But we shouldn't ignore the gifts God has given us to satisfy the Pushy Poppies in our lives.

Bottom line—you'd be immensely disappointed if you asked me to cater a three-course meal for a special event. But if you need me to wash the dishes, I can say *yes* to that.

Signed,
Johnnie Alexander

ABOUT THE AUTHOR

Johnnie Alexander is an award-winning, bestselling novelist of more than thirty works of fiction in a variety of genres. She is both traditionally and indie-published, serves as board secretary for the Mosaic Collection, LLC (an indie-author group) and faculty chair for the Mid-South Christian Writers Conference, cohosts Writers Chat, a weekly online show, and contributes to the HHHistory.com blog.

With a heart for making memories, Johnnie is a fan of classic movies, stacks of books, and road trips. She shares a life of quiet adventure with Rugby, her raccoon-treeing papillon.

TRUTH BEHIND THE FICTION

Kellas Cat

Big Foot. The Loch Ness Monster. The Kellas Cat.

At one time, the rare sightings of a feral, dog-sized, black feline in the Scottish Highlands were treated with the same disdain as sightings of a Himalayan yeti.

Then, in 1983, the male of an adult pair was shot, killed, and taken to a taxidermist to be stuffed. This occurred near a village called Kellas in Morayshire—thus the name given to the species.

Known as the Tomas Christie Kellas Cat, this specimen measured about fifteen inches at the shoulder—the height of an average Shetland Sheepdog—and measured forty-two to forty-three inches from nose to tail. That's nearly four feet long! The tail adds about twelve more inches to the length.

The Tomas Christie Kellas Cat is now exhibited at the Elgin Museum, Scotland's oldest independent museum.

Over the next few years, gamekeepers shot or snared more of the cats. A blood sample from a female trapped near Kellas in 1986 was sent to Aberdeen University's Zoology Department. The chromosomal analysis proved the cat was a cross between a Scottish wildcat and domestic cat. This is considered an interspecific hybrid—the same as the offspring of a horse and a donkey or a lion and a tiger. Unlike a mule, however, the Kellas cat isn't necessarily sterile.

Researchers don't consider the Kellas a formal cat breed like a Siamese or a Persian. They also have the feral instincts of their wildcat parent. This is true even of Kellas cats who are born in captivity.

It's very likely that Martha Banks will need to release Hagar and her kittens, once they're old enough, into the wild.

YORKSHIRE YUMMIES

Yorkshire Parkin

Ingredients:

1¾ sticks unsalted butter
½ cup turbinado sugar or dark brown sugar
¼ cup dark molasses
½ cup golden syrup (also known as light treacle; this is *not* corn syrup; recipe below.)
1½ cups dry oats
1½ cups self-rising flour
¾ teaspoon baking powder
3 teaspoons ground ginger
2 tablespoons milk
2 large eggs, slightly beaten

Directions:
1. Preheat oven to 350 degrees.
2. Grease and line 8x8 baking pan.
3. Combine butter, brown sugar, molasses, and golden syrup in saucepan.
4. Simmer over low heat until sugar and butter are melted. Set aside to cool.
5. Combine dry ingredients.
6. Add cooled mixture to dry ingredients; mix well.
7. Stir in milk.

8. Gradually add eggs and combine. (Be careful not to scramble the eggs!)
9. Pour batter into pan.
10. Bake for 35 to 45 minutes or until a toothpick comes out clean.
11. Cool for about fifteen minutes before removing from pan.
12. **Note:** The Yorkshire Parkin gets better with age and will stay fresh for two to five days if placed in an airtight container.

Golden Syrup

Ingredients:

½ cup water

2 cups sugar

1 tablespoon lemon juice

(preferably fresh)

Directions:

1. Combine water and sugar in saucepan. Gently stir until mixture boils.
2. Add lemon juice.
3. Reduce heat and simmer, uncovered, until mixture is a rich golden color (about 40 to 60 minutes) or until temperature reaches 240 to 250 degrees. DO NOT STIR.
4. After syrup cools a few minutes, pour it into a glass jar.
5. Once syrup is completely cool, close the jar with a tight-sealing lid.
6. Store at room temperature.
7. **Note:** If the syrup thickens too much, reheat and add a little water. If the syrup is too thin, boil mixture a little longer.

Read on for a sneak peek of another exciting book in the Mysteries of Cobble Hill Farm *series!*

The Elephant in the Room
BY SANDRA ORCHARD

Basking in the unusually warm November morning, Harriet Bailey-Knight reclined in her patio chair in the garden and tilted her face toward the sun. "To be honest, I don't understand the appeal. A member of the nobility is the last thing I'd want to be."

"You'll always be a lady to me." Harriet's husband, Will, handed her a cup of tea, his tone affectionate.

Her hand wobbled, spilling her tea into the saucer beneath, as if to prove how non-noble she was. "You know what I mean." Living up to her grandfather's reputation as an excellent veterinarian when she first moved to Yorkshire had been hard enough. "I'd hate the social pressure members of the peerage face. Everyone would always expect every hair to be in place and that I'd wear the latest fashions. All the ladies wear those fancy hats. I don't look good in hats."

"You look beautiful whatever you're wearing."

She laughed. "You're just saying that because I made breakfast." And realizing how perfectly he'd made her point, she straightened in her chair. "See, that's the other thing that would bother me—

never knowing if someone was pandering to me because of what I could do for them."

Will's eyes twinkled in that way they always did when he had her cornered. "Trust me. You making breakfast is just a bonus."

Chuckling, Harriet leaned across the table and kissed him.

Harriet's assistant, Polly Worthington, appeared in the garden. "All right if I interrupt?"

Will gave Harriet a peck on the cheek then pushed to his feet. "She's all yours. I need to go if I want to make this conference before the opening assembly."

Harriet stood and gave Will a proper hug, inhaling the comforting, woodsy scent of his aftershave. "I'll miss you. Drive carefully."

"I'll miss you too, but I'll be back before you know it." After a last kiss, he strolled away.

Polly helped herself to a cup of tea from the pot on the patio table and sat across from Harriet's chair. "You two are still like newlyweds," she teased when Harriet rejoined her. "So cute."

"This from the woman who's been married—what? A month and a half longer than I have?"

"That's right. Your voice of experience."

Grinning, Harriet picked up the toy Maxwell dropped at her feet. The little dachshund had to maneuver about the yard with a wheeled prothesis her grandfather had fitted for him to compensate for his paralyzed back legs, so Harriet tossed the toy only a couple of yards.

"Forgive me for being nosy." Polly swept her hair into a loose knot at the nape of her neck. "But who are you worried is pandering to you?"

"Oh, that. Ever since Will's dad befriended Sir Bruce and then discovered he was a long-lost relative, nobility seems to be a topic that comes up every time Gordon and Will talk. I was telling Will I don't understand why his dad is so psyched about being related to a baronet."

"Seriously?" Disbelief pitched Polly's voice higher.

Harriet rolled her eyes. "Not you too."

"Don't tell me you've never dreamed of having a handsome prince sweep you off your feet." Polly took Ash Wednesday, the gray kitten Will had adopted, into her arms and cuddled him.

"I tended to dream more about horses, dogs, and cats."

As if taking the pronouncement as an invitation, Charlie, the clinic's resident cat, jumped into Harriet's lap, purring loudly as she nestled in.

Polly gave an unladylike snort. "Not me. I loved to play dress-up. Mum would let me wear her wedding veil, and I'd pretend I was a princess." Polly brought her teacup to her lips with an exaggerated lift of her pinky finger.

Harriet burst out laughing.

Polly laid a hand on her chest as if affronted. "I'll have you know my mum worked in a manor house before she married Dad. And she took great pains to teach me proper etiquette in case I should ever be invited to dine with royalty."

"And your brothers?" Harriet deadpanned, recalling their rough-around-the-edges demeanor at her wedding reception.

Polly swept their behavior aside with a flick of her hand. "Lost cause. But I'd be happy to give you a few tips before your speech at Lady Miltshire's brunch next Saturday."

Harriet groaned. "You'll make me a nervous wreck—more than I already am." When Lady Miltshire had first asked her to speak at the fundraiser for rehoming retired racehorses, she'd felt honored. But the more time she'd had to think about it, the more anxious she'd grown.

Polly obliged Maxwell with a ball toss when he brought it to her. "So, your father-in-law is still into his ancestry research, is he?"

"Oh yes. He called again last night with his latest findings."

"I imagine the research is fun for him. Don't we all harbor a secret dream that if we give the old family tree a good shake, a long-lost estate or title of a wealthy ancestor will fall into our laps?"

Harriet's cheeks heated at the realization she'd been blessed with such a gift in the generous bequest of her grandfather, who'd left her Cobble Hill Farm, complete with his veterinary practice, home, and art gallery.

The sound of a car rumbling up the drive drew Harriet's attention to the time. She sprang to her feet, unceremoniously dropping Charlie to the ground, and called Maxwell. "We'd better get to the clinic. Sounds as if our first client is here."

Despite his handicap, Maxwell quickly led the way inside.

Polly collected the teapot and milk jug and fell into step behind them. "Your first client is Roger and his rottweiler. Her pups are due in two weeks, and he's become a nervous Nellie."

By the time Harriet had seen to Roger's dog—whose pregnancy was progressing smoothly—two other dogs, and the Yateses' budgie, Griffen, Polly had a short list of farm calls waiting.

"I rescheduled your one o'clock appointment for four, so you should have plenty of time to attend all three emergencies."

"Since it's Friday, why don't I pay Nancy and Rover a house call after the farm visits instead of them coming here? That way you can have the afternoon off."

"That's okay. I've been overhauling the files and want to get them finished."

"Are you sure?"

"You know me once I set my mind to organizing something."

"Yes, I do." Polly was the most organized person Harriet knew. Harriet read through the list Polly gave her and noted that *Castlegate Manor* was written at the top. "Are these listed in order of urgency?"

"Probably not. But the Castlegates aren't a family that likes to be kept waiting."

Harriet grimaced. Thankfully, no one at the estate had ever complained about her services. "This will be my first visit since Lord Castlegate passed."

"Oh, there's a new lord of the manor now." Polly donned a comically posh accent. "His Lordship's son, Clifford. He's the same age as me. I saw him at our secondary school reunion last weekend."

"He moved away after school?" Harriet asked.

"Actually, he only attended the local school for a year before his father shipped him off to boarding school. But of course everyone remembers him, being the son of a lord and all. And his sister, Edwina, stayed here. She was a year behind us."

"Why would their father send one off to boarding school and not the other?"

"Clifford was a bit of a prankster. But I'm pretty sure his father sent him away to thwart his romance with Maisie Coop. You know her as Maisie Aubert."

"Really?" Harriet widened her eyes in surprise that a chicken farmer would have turned the head of a lord's son. But maybe she wasn't a farmer at the time.

"They were inseparable. Until his dad intervened, that is. Although, judging by the way Clifford spoke to her at the reunion, he clearly thought their love should have survived."

"He said that to her? In front of everyone?"

"I doubt Clifford was paying any attention to the rest of us listening in." Polly's eyes twinkled with mischief. "He said he'd written to her faithfully for months, and it was obvious he was peeved that Maisie hadn't bothered to send a single reply. Although she claimed she had."

"That must have been uncomfortable for her and Pierre." Maisie's husband was fairly new to their community, having moved from France only a few years before to open a leather goods shop.

"Thankfully, Pierre wasn't there. It would've been very embarrassing for him, especially after Clifford came back to Maisie and apologized. He said he'd lashed out because it had hurt not hearing from her all those years ago. Then he kissed her hand and held it to his heart and declared that he'd never stopped caring about her."

Harriet winced. She didn't know Pierre well, having only chatted briefly with him now and again at church, but Clifford's behavior would have been upsetting for any husband.

"Maisie must have wondered how her life could have played out if she'd waited for Clifford," Polly went on. "But after his confession, she looked even more uncomfortable and made a quick exit."

"Didn't Clifford know she was married?"

"Someone told him after she left. You should've seen his face." Polly whistled.

"Yes, I can imagine. Anyway, I'd better get moving on the farm calls."

Fifteen minutes later, Harriet parked her grandfather's old Land Rover, which she'd affectionately dubbed the Beast, next to her client's shiny new BMW.

Edwina Castlegate trotted from the field on a lively bay and met Harriet outside the stables. She alighted from the horse in one graceful movement and handed her reins to a groom then removed her riding helmet and shook out her long blond waves. Even in riding chaps and a light jacket, she looked as if she'd stepped off the pages of a fashion magazine, without so much as a hint of helmet head.

Harriet shook away the whimsical thought. "Is Thunder in here?"

"Yes." Edwina's voice quivered. She had a reputation for being passionate about her horses and clearly hated seeing them suffer. "I'd planned to exercise him this morning, but the groom noticed he was favoring his left hind leg."

"Let's have a look then."

The groom had the gelding in the barn's brightly lit center aisle. Thunder shifted his weight, and Harriet could see he was favoring his leg, just as Edwina had said.

Speaking to the horse in a gentle tone, Harriet skimmed her hand along his flank and down his leg before coaxing him to lift his foot for her. He did so willingly. She extended her free hand to the groomsman. "Could you hand me a hoof pick, please?"

He handed her the most beautiful horse pick she'd ever seen. The pick's end was polished to a high gleam, and the handle, made of wood inlaid with mother-of-pearl, fit perfectly in her grip. The Castlegates clearly didn't skimp on quality or aesthetics.

Harriet cleaned out what little dirt still clung to the hoof and gingerly poked around in search of tender spots. In the same way a person could bruise a foot if they stepped wrong on something hard, horses could too. And if that was the case, Thunder might favor the sore spot for weeks. But that didn't appear to be his problem. "Would you please walk him for me?"

While moving, Thunder's lameness was noticeable but mild. Harriet turned to Edwina. "When you last exercised him, did you detect a change in his gait? Or difficulty with transitions or with stopping?"

"Yes. He's been a bit off for the last couple of days." Edwina's gloved hands rested lightly on her hips as she scrunched her nose. "It's why I wanted to work with him more."

"Has he fallen recently?" Harriet motioned to the groom to turn the horse and bring him toward her.

"We took a tumble a fortnight ago, but we both got right back up and carried on."

Harriet palpated the horse's pelvis. "Please secure him, and I'll bring in my portable X-ray machine to take a few pictures. He could have a fracture."

Edwina's cheeks paled. Then she buried her face against the horse's neck and whispered apologies. His glossy coat shone like burnished copper, testimony to how well cared for he was.

As Harriet joined them in the barn with her diagnostic equipment, a young woman scurried across the drive toward them. "Is His Lordship in the stables?"

"No, he's speaking to that man who's redesigning the gazebo," Edwina said. "Why?"

"There's a foreign gentleman waiting in his office to speak to him."

"Did you get his name?" Edwina snapped.

"Yes, milady. Mr. Aubert, the man from the leather shop. I served him tea and had him wait in His Lordship's office."

Edwina's eyes flashed. "You left a tradesman unattended in the house?" She turned to Harriet. "Excuse me. I need to see to this." To the young woman, she added, "No need to bother my brother."

The pair strode off, and Harriet shook her head over the stark contrast between the woman's treatment of her beloved horse and how she treated her staff. Where Edwina's obvious bond with her horse had warmed Harriet's heart, Harriet doubted one would ever catch Her Ladyship apologizing to a servant.

With the groom's capable assistance, Harriet x-rayed the leg. "How bad does it look, miss?" he asked as she studied the images.

"It's not broken or dislocated. I suspect he's strained a ligament." She went over the area again. "There are definite signs of inflammation." She unpacked the ultrasound machine she'd also retrieved from the Beast. "This will give us a better picture of the ligaments."

Someone approached and stopped behind her, casting a shadow across Harriet's screen. "What's all this?" a man's voice asked.

She squinted up to find a handsome, blond-haired man about ten years her junior studying her. "You must be the new lord of the manor." The family resemblance was undeniable.

He extended his hand and shook hers in a firm grip. "Clifford Castlegate. And you're Old Doc Bailey's granddaughter, I presume."

"That's right. Dr. Harriet Bailey-Knight."

"Ah yes, Harriet. I remember you coming here a time or two when I was a kid."

"Yes, when I was a teenager. I'm surprised you remember."

He tapped his head. "I have a mind like an elephant's. Never forget. I heard you took over your grandfather's practice."

"About a year and a half ago."

Clifford nodded and motioned to Thunder. "And what's the matter with my sister's horse?" Before Harriet could explain, he added, "Where is she, by the way? It's unlike her not to be on hand when her horses are being seen to." This last part he directed to the groom.

"She had to deal with a tradesman, sir."

Clifford chuckled. "Leave it to Edwina to put unsolicited tradesmen in their place." He shifted his attention to the image on the ultrasound screen. "What are we looking at here?"

"I'm assessing the ligaments." Satisfied that the ultrasound images corroborated her theory, Harriet excused herself to retrieve the appropriate medication from her vehicle, hoping Edwina would return soon. With two more farmers waiting for her services, she didn't have time to go over her findings and care instructions twice.

Once outside, she spotted an irate Pierre Aubert tromping out of the manor house carrying a leather duffel bag. When he reached his car, he cast a furtive glance over his shoulder, shoved the bag into his trunk, and sped off.

Harriet wondered about his behavior as she carried the injection back to where Clifford and the groom waited with Thunder in the barn.

"What's the needle for?" Clifford asked.

"Inflammation. It should also help with pain. In fact, if you'll give me a hand by holding the ultrasound paddle right here"—Harriet moved the instrument into position—"I'll be able to see where the needle is going and inject the medicine precisely where it will be most effective."

Clifford's gaze was fixed on the screen. "Amazing."

With the injection finished, Harriet retrieved the paddle from Clifford and told the groom he could return Thunder to his box.

Edwina joined them at the stable door, muttering about the impertinence of tradesmen.

"Who was it? What did he want?" her brother asked.

"The owner of that new custom leather goods and repair shop." Irritation laced Edwina's tone. "Presumably to drum up more business. I don't know. I didn't give him a chance to make his pitch."

Clifford squinted down the drive in the direction the tradesman had disappeared. "Maisie's husband came to see us?"

Stiffening, Edwina crossed her arms. "Yes."

Clifford scratched his chin. "I wish you hadn't sent him away. I would have liked to meet him." Without waiting for Edwina's response, he strode toward the house.

Edwina huffed. "You'd think he'd be grateful I got rid of the man before he could make a scene. I still can't believe he canceled his weekend trip to Paris last week in favor of the school reunion."

Harriet wasn't sure if Edwina expected a response, and glanced at the groom for help, but he merely smirked and carried on with his work. Harriet needed to do the same, but her curiosity got the better of her. "Why would Pierre make a scene?"

Edwina rolled her eyes. "Because my brother is still in love with the man's wife, of course. I suppose since you're new to town, you wouldn't know they used to be sweethearts."

"Lady Edwina, Lady Edwina!" The same maid as before dashed across the lawn, her cheeks flushed. "His Lordship wants you to come straightaway."

"What is it now, Louise?" Edwina practically growled the words.

"The silver elephant statue, milady." Louise wrung her hands in the folds of her apron. "It's gone!"

A NOTE FROM THE EDITORS

We hope you enjoyed another exciting volume in the Mysteries of Cobble Hill Farm series, published by Guideposts. For over seventy-five years, Guideposts, a nonprofit organization, has been driven by a vision of a world filled with hope. We aspire to be the voice of a trusted friend, a friend who makes you feel more hopeful and connected.

By making a purchase from Guideposts, you join our community in touching millions of lives, inspiring them to believe that all things are possible through faith, hope, and prayer. Your continued support allows us to provide uplifting resources to those in need. Whether through our communities, websites, apps, or publications, we inspire our audiences, bring them together, and comfort, uplift, entertain, and guide them. Visit us at guideposts.org to learn more.

We would love to hear from you. Write us at Guideposts, P.O. Box 5815, Harlan, Iowa 51593 or call us at (800) 932-2145. Did you love *Pride, Prejudice, and Pitfalls*? Leave a review for this product on guideposts.org/shop. Your feedback helps others in our community find relevant products.

Find inspiration, find faith, find Guideposts.
Shop our best sellers and favorites at
guideposts.org/shop
Or scan the QR code to go directly to our Shop.

Loved Mysteries of Cobble Hill Farm? Check out some other Guideposts mystery series! Visit https://www.shopguideposts.org/fiction-books/mystery-fiction.html for more information.

SECRETS FROM GRANDMA'S ATTIC

Life is recorded not only in decades or years, but in events and memories that form the fabric of our being. Follow Tracy Doyle, Amy Allen, and Robin Davisson, the granddaughters of the recently deceased centenarian, Pearl Allen, as they explore the treasures found in the attic of Grandma Pearl's Victorian home, nestled near the banks of the Mississippi in Canton, Missouri. Not only do Pearl's descendants uncover a long-buried mystery at every attic exploration, they also discover their grandmother's legacy of deep, abiding faith, which has shaped and guided their family through the years. These uncovered Secrets from Grandma's Attic reveal stories of faith, redemption, and second chances that capture your heart long after you turn the last page.

History Lost and Found
The Art of Deception
Testament to a Patriot
Buttoned Up

MYSTERIES OF COBBLE HILL FARM

Pearl of Great Price
Hidden Riches
Movers and Shakers
The Eye of the Cat
Refined by Fire
The Prince and the Popper
Something Shady
Duel Threat
A Royal Tea
The Heart of a Hero
Fractured Beauty
A Shadowy Past
In Its Time
Nothing Gold Can Stay
The Cameo Clue
Veiled Intentions
Turn Back the Dial
A Marathon of Kindness
A Thief in the Night
Coming Home

More Great Mysteries Are Waiting for Readers Like *You*!

Whistle Stop Café

"Memories of a lifetime...I loved reading this story. Could not put the book down...." —ROSE H.

Mystery and WWII historical fiction fans will love these intriguing novels where two close friends piece together clues to solve mysteries past and present. Set in the real town of Dennison, Ohio, at a historic train depot where many soldiers set off for war, these stories are filled with faithful, relatable characters you'll love spending time with.

Extraordinary Women of the Bible

"This entire series is a wonderful read.... Gives you a better understanding of the Bible." —SHARON A.

Now, in these riveting stories, you can get to know the most extraordinary women of the Bible, from Rahab and Esther to Bathsheba, Ruth, and more. Each book perfectly combines biblical facts with imaginative storylines to bring these women to vivid life and lets you witness their roles in God's great plan. These stories reveal how we can find the courage and faith needed today to face life's trials and put our trust in God just as they did.

Secrets of Grandma's Attic

"I'm hooked from beginning to end. I love how faith, hope, and prayer are included...[and] the scripture references... in the book at the appropriate time each character needs help. —JACQUELINE

Take a refreshing step back in time to the real-life town of Canton, Missouri, to the late Pearl Allen's home. Hours of page-turning intrigue unfold as her granddaughters uncover family secrets and treasures in their grandma's attic. You'll love seeing how faith has helped shape Pearl's family for generations.

Learn More & Shop These Exciting Mysteries, Biblical Stories & Other Uplifting Fiction at **guideposts.org/fiction**